D0572138

Quick & Easy
THAI
CUISINE
LEMON GRASS COOKBOOK

Distributors:

UNITED STATES: Kodansha America, Inc., through Oxford University Press, 198 Madison Avenue, New York, NY 10016

CANADA: Fitzhenry & Whiteside Ltd., 195 Allstate Parkway, Markham, Ontario L3R 4T8

UNITED KINGDOM AND EUROPE: Premier Book Marketing Ltd., Clarendon House, 52, Cornmarket Street, Oxford, OX1 3HJ England

AUSTRALIA AND NEW ZEALAND: Bookwise International, 174 Cormack Road, Wingfield, SA 5013 Australia

JAPAN: Japan Publications Trading Co., Ltd., 1-2-1, Sarugaku-cho, Chiyoda-ku, Tokyo, 101-0064 Japan

2nd Printing April 2003
 Published by JOIE, INC. 1-8-3, Hirakawa-cho, Chiyoda-ku, Tokyo 102-0093 Japan Printed in Hong Kong

INTRODUCTION

The foods of Thailand consist of many combinations and blends of different flavors, herbs, spices and peppers. It is a fiery cuisine which has become very popular due to the many Thai restaurants offering dishes that are appreciated by the adventurous and sophisticated palates of so many people of today.

Thai cooking has been influenced by Thailand's neighbors, including Burma, India, Laos and Malaysia. Also coloring Thai cuisine are countries such as China and Portugal. The versatility of the Thai people enabled them to refine this variety of traditions to develop one of the most beautiful and flavorful cuisines in the world.

Thai cuisine offers not only well balanced flavors but also the unforgettable fire of peppers (prig kee noo), which makes this style of cooking very addictive. The rich and varied sauces make each dish distinctive and unique.

With the increasing availability of Thai ingredients in the market, Thai cooking can be enjoyed in the home. Employing a variety of fresh seafood, vegetables and *tofu*, Thai cooking is one of healthiest and most nutritious ways to enjoy meals that are quick and easy to prepare.

This book offers a collection of recipes from dishes served in restaurants that were owned and operated in Thailand by Chef Rut's mother. Many of the dishes are also found on the menu of Chef Rut's restaurants in the United States. The easy-to-follow instructions and step-by-step photographs will yield dishes that are as authentic as any found in Thailand.

ACKNOWLEDGMENTS

——Dedicated to our mother.——

I have been blessed by the special love of my mother, whose teachings I have carried with me all my life. Her teachings have shaped my goals and dreams; her patient manner and words of encouragement have helped carry me forward. She always made learning a joyful experience. Her family recipes, so popular in her restaurants in Thailand, were given to me to share, for it is the sharing that brings the most joy to all of us.

I want to thank Steve and my sister Lee Cole for my first opportunity in America, Gordon and my sister Maliwal Hugo for their constant encouragement.

To my brothers, Buncha and Rex Poladitmontri, my most loving thank you for their steadfast support as we progress into further ventures, knowing that our goals remain the same.

My very fondest feelings of gratitude to Charlie and Sandy Hilf, Eric Hilf and Chuck Daniel for the evenings spent with me at my restaurants. They are always supporting and encouraging me with their exceptional friendship, which I will always hold in high regard.

To my special friends John and Penny, and Joe and Joan, my most sincere appreciation for their dedication, patience and belief in me. With their constant devotion, my achievements are even more special to me.

I would also like to thank Mr. Don Scott, whose commitment to our success has always been sincere. This cookbook would not have been possible without his patience and belief in our business. He has our fondest respect and holds a special place in our heart.

To Mr. Shiro Shimura, our publisher, I sincerely thank you for the opportunity to share with everyone the recipes in this book. Thank you for this beginning and the future that we will share.

A special place is always reserved for my friend, Ms. Yukiko Moriyama, for she is responsible for this project. Her patient words of encouragement have helped sustain us. To Yukiko-san, thank you for your help now and in the future.

A very special thank you to Ms. Sumiko Kobayashi for her hard work and dedication to this book. Also, a sincere thank you to Mr. Narahara, Mr. Naito and everyone at JOIE. Inc. for their involvement in this book.

Our deepest gratitude and respect to Mr. Tomio Moriguchi, president of Uwajimaya Inc. of Seattle, Washington, and Ms. Tomoko Matsuno for the opportunity to teach Thai cuisine at the Uwajimaya Cooking School.

A special thank you to Hisayo Nakahara for all the assistance she so graciously provided as she worked with me in anticipating my every move in my cooking classes.

To our friend, George Nakauye, whose patience and sense of design are much appreciated in the completion of this project.

To Grace Locke and David Mar, whose perseverance was indispensable. Your hard work and dedication are very much appreciated and were a key to the success of our projects.

To all of our students and customers, this book is our way of thanking you for your loyalty, which makes this entire project worthwhile.

CONTENTS

CONTENTS

METRIC TABLES

★ 1 cup is equivalent to 240ml in our recipes: (American cup measurement)

1 American cup = 240ml = 8 American fl oz

1 British cup = 200ml = 7 British fl oz

1 Japanese cup = 200ml

1 tablespoon = 15ml   1 teaspoon = 5ml

T = tablespoon	t = teaspoon	C = Cup
fl = fluid	oz = ounce	lb = pound
ml = milliliter	g = gram	cm = centimeter
F = Fahrenheit	C = Celsius	

TABLES CONVERTING FROM U.S. CUSTOMARY SYSTEM TO METRICS

Liquid Measures

U.S. Customary system	oz	g	ml
1/16 cup = 1 T	1/2 oz	14g	15ml
1/4 cup = 4 T	2 oz	60g	59ml
1/2 cup = 8 T	4 oz	115g	118ml
1 cup = 16 T	8 oz	225g	236ml
1 3/4 cups	14 oz	400g	414ml
2 cups = 1 pint	16 oz	450g	473ml
3 cups	24 oz	685g	710ml
4 cups	32 oz	900g	946ml

Liquid Measures

Japanese system	oz	ml
1/8 cup	7/8 oz	25ml
1/4 cup	1 3/4 oz	50ml
1/2 cup	3 1/2 oz	100ml
1 cup	7 oz	200ml
1 1/2 cups	10 1/2 oz	300ml
2 cups	14 oz	400ml
3 cups	21 oz	600ml
4 cups	28 oz	800ml

Weights

ounces to grams *
1/4 oz = 7g
1/2 oz = 14g
1 oz = 30g
2 oz = 60g
4 oz = 115g
6 oz = 170g
8 oz = 225g
16 oz = 450g

* Equivalent

Linear Measures

inches to centimeters
1/2 in = 1.27cm
1 in = 2.54cm
2 in = 5.08cm
4 in = 10.16cm
5 in = 12.7 cm
10 in = 25.4 cm
15 in = 38.1 cm
20 in = 50.8 cm

Temperatures

Fahrenheit (F) to Celsius (C)	
freezer storage	−10°F = −23.3°C
	0°F = −17.7°C
water freezes	32°F = 0 °C
	68°F = 20 °C
	100°F = 37.7°C
water boils	212°F = 100 °C
	300°F = 148.8°C
	400°F = 204.4°C

Deep-Frying Oil Temperatures

300°F − 330°F (150°C − 165°C) = low
340°F − 350°F (170°C − 175°C) = moderate
350°F − 360°F (175°C − 180°C) = high

Conversion Factor

$$C = F - 32 \times 5/9$$

$$F = \frac{C \times 9}{5} + 32$$

BASIC HINTS

1. Read each recipe completely and have all ingredients cut, prepared and measured to make the cooking process flow smoothly.

2. Soak dried rice noodles in cold water (enough to cover them) for two hours, or overnight for best results. For immediate use, soak in warm water for 1/2 hour. Always rinse and drain soaked rice noodles before using them in any recipe.

3. For Thai cooking, use Thai Jasmine rice unless otherwise specified in the recipe.

4. Sticky rice should be soaked for at least one hour in warm water, or overnight in cold water, before cooking in a steamer.

5. To retain the color of the vegetables and the tenderness of the meat, do not use intense high heat when cooking until all ingredients of the recipe are combined.

6. Steam seafoods gently on medium high heat to prevent dryness and over cooking.

7. Always use the freshest vegetables and seafoods available for best results.

8. Keep in mind color, flavor and texture when selecting vegetables for the recipes.

9. Use the best quality Thai fish sauce available for the best flavor and aroma of each dish.

10. Spice mixtures and curry pastes can be prepared ahead of time and stored in the refrigerator or freezer.

11. In general, use only the lower third of the stalk of fresh lemon grass. The top portion is not usually called for in recipes, unless so specified.

12. Taste all dishes before serving to check for the proper balance of flavors.

ไข่ยัดไส้

THAI EGG OMELET

Also delicious for breakfast.

〈INGREDIENTS: 4 servings〉

1/4 lb. (115 g) pork
1/4 lb. (115 g) shrimp, shelled and deveined

1 clove garlic, minced

2 T fish sauce
1 T seasoning sauce
2 T sugar

1 small tomato, diced
1 small onion, diced
1/8 c green beans, chopped or green peas

1/8 c carrots, chopped
1/4 c each red and green bell peppers, chopped
6 eggs, beaten
1/8 t white pepper
3 T oil

cilantro and green onions for garnish

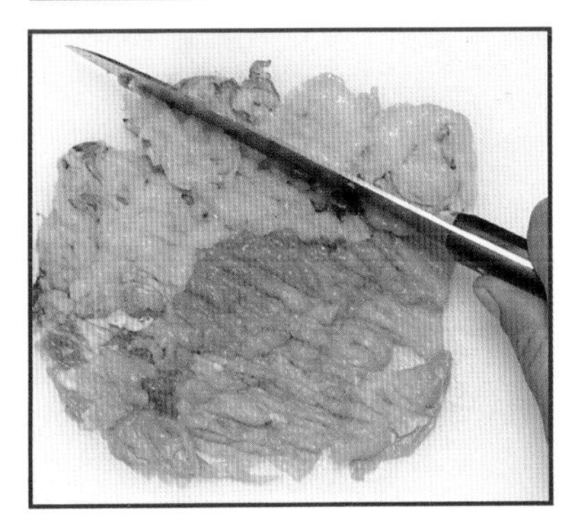

1. Mince pork and shrimp together.

2. Chop all vegetables.

3. Heat a pan and add 1 T of the oil and garlic. Stir fry meat mixture until done.

4. Add fish sauce, seasoning sauce and sugar. Continue to cook until the sauce is reduced. Add all vegetables and stir to combine. Mix white pepper into vegetables.

5. Heat pan on medium heat and coat with a thin layer of oil. Add 1/4 of egg mixture and roll to coat surface of pan. Add 1/4 of filling mixture and allow omelet to cook.

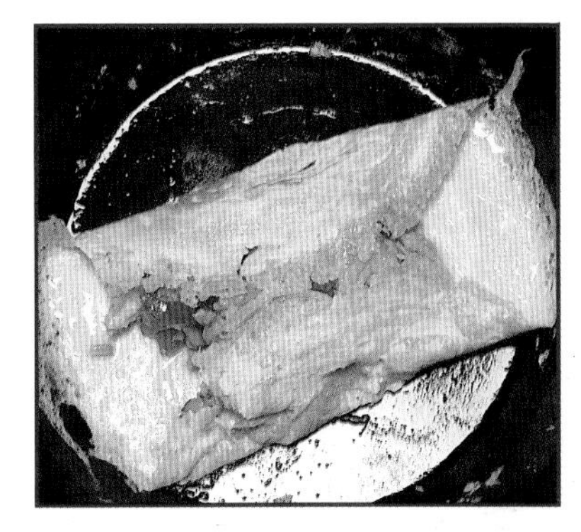

6. Fold 2 sides together.

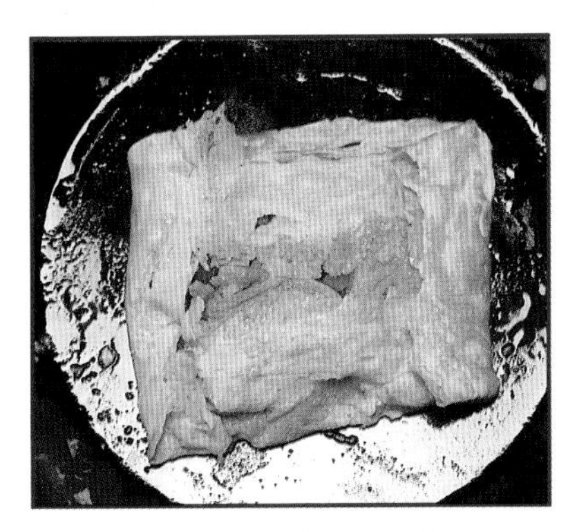

7. Fold other 2 sides together.

8. Place a plate on top of omelet and turn pan upside down to invert omelet, showing the bottom as the top. Continue to make other omelets.

ปอเปี๊ยะทอด

SPRING ROLLS

POR PIA SOD

Serve with a sweet and sour sauce.

〈INGREDIENTS: 4 servings〉

2 T oil
1 t minced garlic
2 c shredded celery
2 c shredded carrot
3 T fish sauce
2 T sugar
1/8 t white pepper
1 egg yolk, beaten (to seal wrappers) (optional)

12 spring roll wrappers

Garnishes: Green leaf lettuce, cucumber and tomato
3 C oil for deep frying (350°F, 175°C)

1. Cut and chop all vegetables.

2. Heat a frying pan; add oil and garlic. Add all vegetables and seasonings. Cook for 1 minute on high heat to reduce sauce. Whatever liquid is left, drain from filling. Allow filling to cool before wrapping. Follow instructions for wrapping.

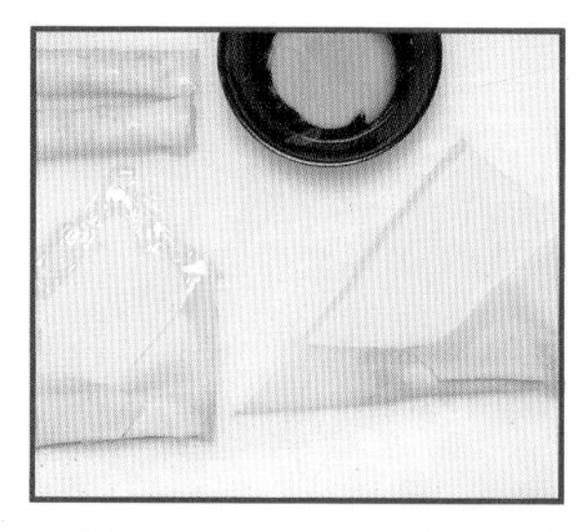

3. Place wrapper as a diamond with corner towards you. Place 2 T filling ingredients in lower portion of wrapper. Fold side up, rolling once. Bring sides in and spread upper portion of wrapper with egg yolk.

4. Roll wrapper up to seal entire spring roll. Deep fry in hot oil until golden brown, turning as needed.

ปอเปี๊ยะสด

FRESH SPRING ROLLS

POR PIA TOD

Serve with peanut sauce.

〈INGREDIENTS: 4 servings〉

3 Chinese sausages, steamed
1 cube fried *tofu*
1 cucumber
2 c beansprouts, blanched
2 c spinach, blanched
4 leaves green leaf lettuce
$^1/_2$ c peanut sauce (see page 61)
12 spring roll wrappers

Granishes: Cilantro and tomato roses

1. Cut Chinese sausage, *tofu* and cucumbers into $^1/_2$ inch (1.5 cm) strips. Have all other ingredients ready and set aside.

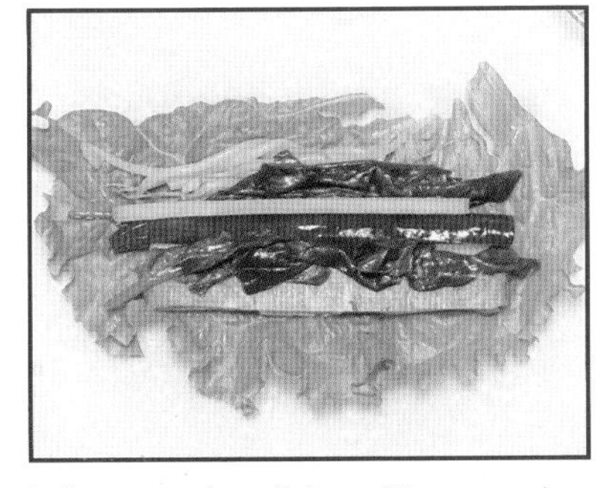

2. Separate spring roll sheets. Place one spring roll sheet on a flat surface. Place one lettuce leaf on lower portion of wrapper. Arrange one piece of Chinese sausage, *tofu*, cucumber and beansprouts on top of lettuce leaf.

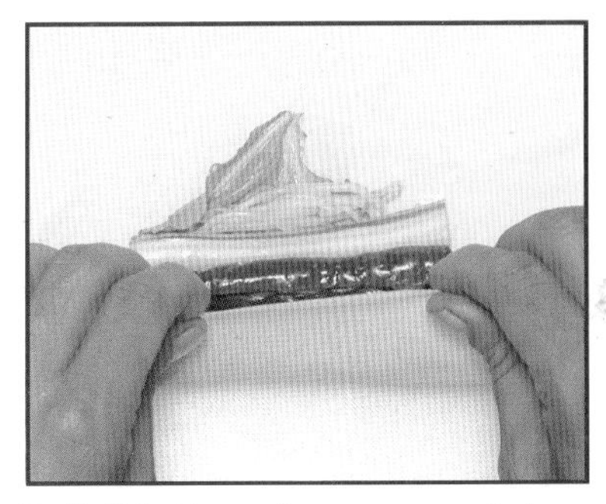

3. Roll bottom of wrapper up, bring sides and continue to roll all the way up. Slice rolls before serving.

ผัดผักเต้าหู้

TOFU WITH VEGETABLES PAD PUG TOA HOO

Other vegetables may be used.

⟨INGREDIENTS: 4 servings⟩

1 T oil
1 clove garlic, minced

1/4 c sliced onions
1/4 c beansprouts
1/4 pea pods
1/4 c sliced carrots
1/4 c sliced red bell peppers
1/4 c sliced cauliflower
1/4 c sliced broccoli

1/4 c sliced mushrooms

2 c fried *tofu* squares

1 T fish sauce
1 T oyster sauce
1 T sugar

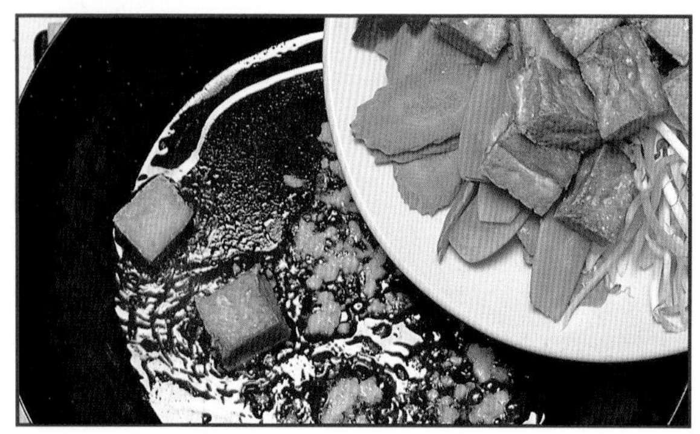

1. Heat pan add oil and garlic. Add all vegetables and fried *tofu*.

2. Add fish sauce, oyster sauce and sugar. Continue to cook slowly for 2 minutes until vegetables are crisp tender.

BEEF SALAD

YUM NUEA

A wonderful steak served with hot steamed rice and any vegetable dish.

〈INGREDIENTS: 4 servings〉

$^1/_2$ lb. (225g) New York steak
1 T fish sauce

Green leaf lettuce

$^1/_2$ tomato sliced into thin pieces
$^1/_2$ c cucumber slices
$^1/_4$ c sliced red and green bell peppers
$^1/_4$ c sliced onions
$^1/_2$ c sliced mushrooms
1 green onion sliced

Dressing:
3 T fish sauce
3 T lime juice
1 T sugar
3 cloves garlic, minced
2 Thai chili peppers

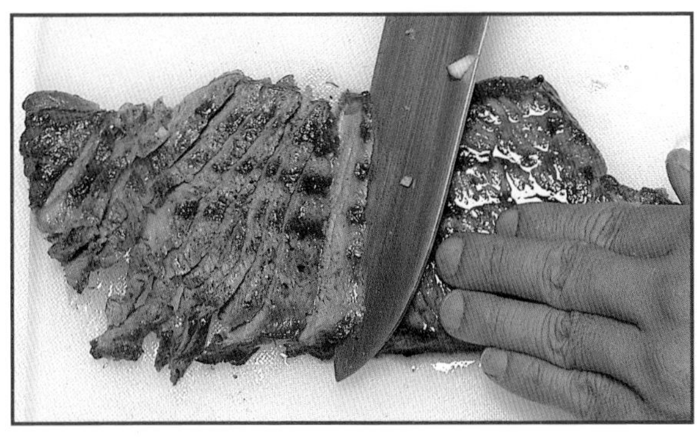

1. Marinate steak with fish sauce for approx. 5 minutes. Grill steak until done to desired degree. Slice and set aside.

2. Line a large platter with green leaf lettuce. Arrange all ingredients on top of lettuce and pour dressing over all ingredients. Garnish with cilantro.

ขนมจีนซาวน้ำ

PINEAPPLE NOODLE SALAD

This dish is good as a summer salad.

〈INGREDIENTS: 4 servings〉

1/2 lb. (225 g) thin noodles (*somen* noodles)

1/2 lb. (225 g) shrimp
1/2 c coconut cream

1/4 c crushed pineapple
5 cloves garlic, peeled and chopped
2 T slivered fresh ginger root

Dressing:
1/4 c fresh lime juice
1/4 c fish sauce
2 T sugar

Garnishes: Slivered red bell pepper and slices of lime and green onions

1. Boil noodles for 3 minutes.

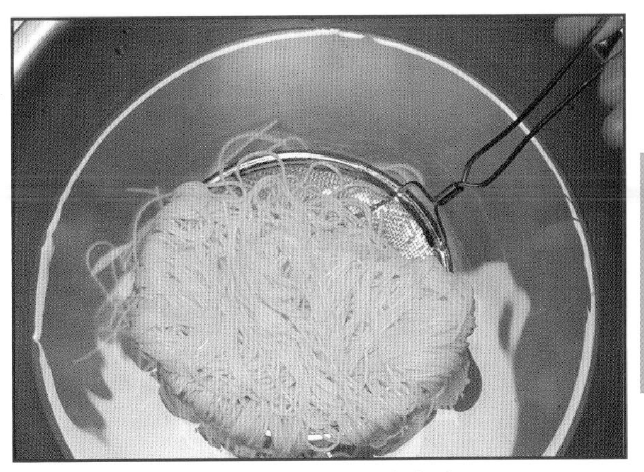

2. Rinse noodles in cold water and drain.

3. Shell and devein shrimp. Quickly cook shrimp in coconut cream.

4. Arrange pineapple and all other ingredients along with noodles on a platter.

5. Top with shrimp mixture. Prepare dressing and pour over noodles. Garnish with peppers, lime and green onions.

GREEN CURRY PASTE

10	whole fresh jalapeno chili peppers
5	whole Thai chili
1/2 c	coriander root or stems
8	cloves garlic
1/4 c	chopped shallots (or purple onions)
1/4 c	chopped lemon grass (or 1 T dried lemon grass)
5	sliced fresh galanga (or 1 t dried galanga powder (loas))
1 t	cumin
1 t	shrimp paste

Combine all ingredients in a blender and process until smooth.

ส้มตำมะละกอ

THAI PAPAYA SALAD

SOMTUMMALAGOR

When papaya is not available, cabbage can be used as a substitute.

〈INGREDIENTS: 4 servings〉

- 1 medium Thai green papaya
- 1 carrot, shredded
- 1 tomato, cut into wedges
- 1/4 c ground roasted peanuts
- 1/4 c dried shrimp, soaked for 5 minutes in warm water
- 1/2 c lime juice
- 1/3 c fish sauce
- 3 T sugar
- 1 large clove garlic, minced

Garnishes: Lime slices, chili pepper

1/4 head cabbage, shredded (use if papaya is not available).

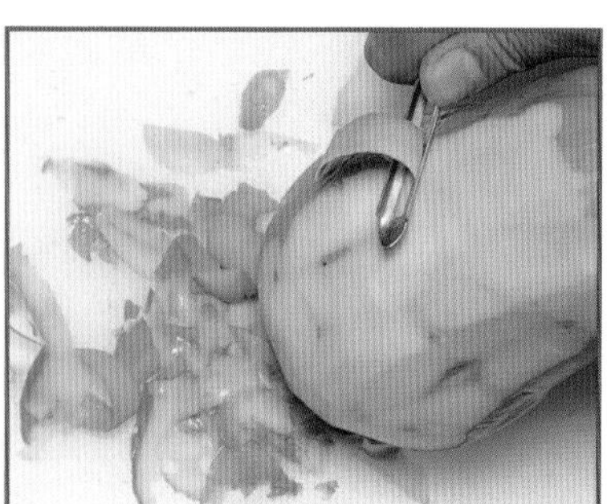

1. Peel and seed papaya.

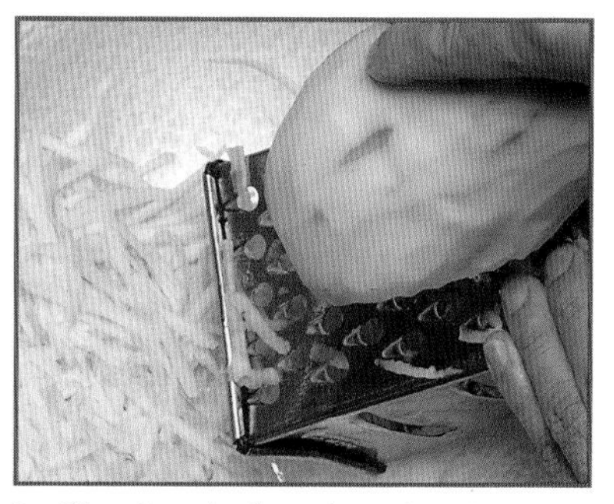

2. Shred and place in a bowl.

3. Add all remaining ingredients and thoroughly mix before serving.

ลาบไก่

NORTHERN CHICKEN SALAD LAAB GAI

Good served with sticky rice and heaven beef.

⟨INGREDIENTS: 4 servings⟩

1 lb. (225g) ground chicken breast

Sauce:
- 5 T lime juice
- 1/4 c fish sauce
- 1/2 t ground chili pepper
- 2 T minced onion
- 1/2 t galanga powder

- 1 T ground toasted sweet rice
- 1/8 c chopped green onions
- 1/8 c fresh mint leaves
- 1/8 c chopped cilantro

Garnishes:
Sliced red cabbage, green leaf lettuce, fresh pea pods, sliced carrots, green bell pepper and red bell pepper

NOTE: *Toasted rice: Toast sweet rice in a skillet on medium heat until light brown. Remove and process in a blender until a fine mixture is formed.*

1. Combine chicken and sauce ingredients in a pan and cook chicken until done.

2. Add toasted rice, green onions, mint leaves and cilantro. Garnish chicken before serving.

ยำหอยกุยดั๊ค

GEODUCK CLAM SALAD

A delicious first course or serve as a complete light meal.

〈INGREDIENTS: 4 servings〉

1/2 lb.(225g) thinly sliced geoduck clam (neck portion only)
1 t cornstarch
1 t white wine
1 clove garlic, minced
1 t grated fresh ginger root

1 T oil

2 c shredded lettuce
1/4 c sliced red bell pepper
1/4 c sliced green bell pepper
1/4 c sliced fresh mushrooms
1/4 c sliced fresh pea pods
1/4 c sliced fresh onions
1/8 c fresh mint leaves
1/4 c sliced fresh lemon grass
1 tomato cut into wedges
1/4 cucumber slices

Sauce:
1 t red curry paste
1 t minced fresh garlic
1/4 c fresh lime juice
1/4 c fish sauce
2 T sugar

Optional garnishes:
1 T ground roasted minced sweet rice
1/4 c minced fresh cilantro
1/2 sliced green onions and cilantro for garnish

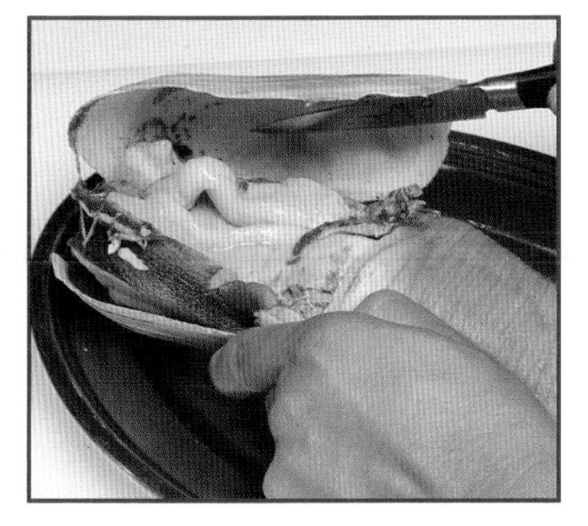

1. Clean geoduck clam and use neck portion only reserving other portion for another use.

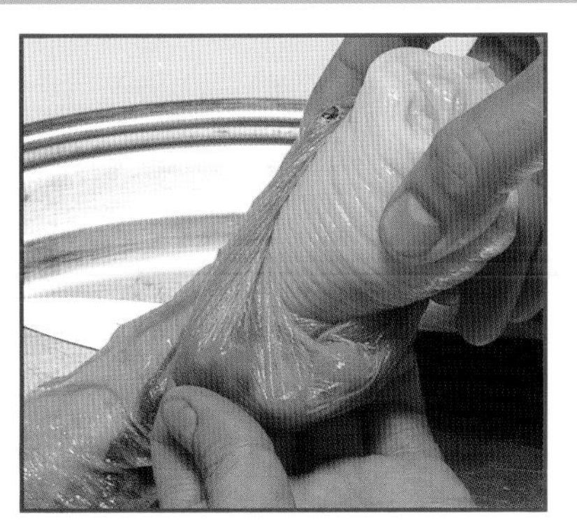

2. Rinse carefully to remove sand and skin.

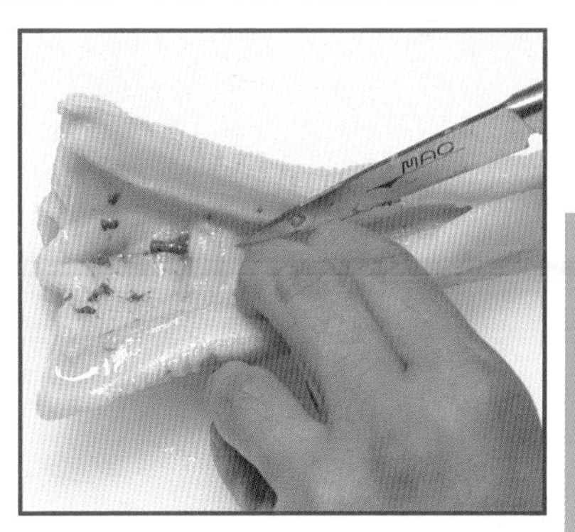

3. Cut off the very tip of the neck and slice open lengthwise.

4. Slice neck portion into thin slices.

5. Marinate geoduck slices in cornstarch and white wine, garlic and ginger.

6. Heat frying pan, add oil. Saute geoduck quickly and remove. Set aside.

7. Prepare all other ingredients and sauce.

8. Combine geoduck slices with sliced vegetables and toss with dressing just before serving. Garnish with sliced green onions and cilantro.

พล่ากุ้ง

LEMON GRASS SHRIMP SALAD PLA GOONG

Sauté shrimp in pan with a small amount of white wine and basil to give a nice flavor.

〈INGREDIENTS: 4 servings〉

Dressing:

- 1 T Grand Palace Red Curry Paste
- 6 T lime juice
- 4 T fish sauce
- 2 T sugar
- 1 T chopped lemon grass

- 1 lb. (450g) medium shrimp, shelled and deveined
- 2 c sliced romaine lettuce
- 1/4 c sliced red bell pepper
- 1/2 c sliced cucumber
- 1/2 c sliced carrots
- 1/2 c sliced onions
- 1 tomato cut in wedges
- 1/4 c mint leaves
- 1/4 c sliced green bell pepper
- 1/4 c sliced mushrooms
- 1/4 c fresh pea pods
- 1/4 c chopped cilantro
- 1 green onion, chopped

1. Prepare dressing and set aside.

2. Grill or boil shrimp to cook, set aside. Toss remaining ingredients with shrimp and place on a platter. Garnish with cilantro and green onions.

ข้าวต้มกุ้ง

RICE SOUP

KHOW TOM GOONG

A delicious breakfast soup or light snack.

⟨INGREDIENTS: 4 servings⟩

- 2 c water
- 1 T seasoning sauce
- 1/4 t white pepper
- 1/2 t galanga powder
- 2 stalks celery, chopped

- 1/2 lb. (225g) shrimp, shelled, deveined and butterflied
- 1 c cooked white rice
- 2 T fish sauce

- 2 T oil
- 1 t minced garlic

cilantro for garnish

1. Bring water to a boil and add seasoning sauce, white pepper, galanga powder and chopped celery.

2. Add shrimp.

3. Add rice and fish sauce. Bring to a boil and cook for 3 minutes.

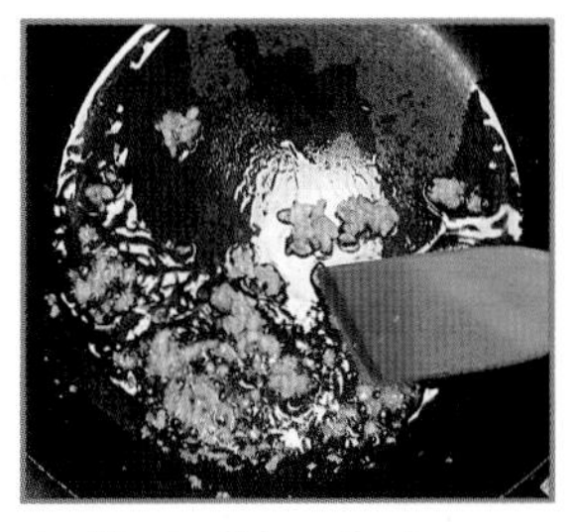

4. Heat oil in a frying pan and fry garlic on medium high heat until golden brown. Serve the fried garlic with the rice soup.

ต้มยำกุ้ง

SPICY SHRIMP SOUP

TOM YUM GOONG

The most famous soup of Thai cuisine.

〈INGREDIENTS: 4 servings〉

- 1/2 lb. (225 g) prawns, shelled, deveined (reserve shells)
- 4 c water
- 1/2 c sliced fresh mushrooms

Sauce:

- 2 cloves garlic, minced
- 5 kaffir lime leaves
- 6 T lime juice
- 6 T fish sauce
- 1 stalk lemon grass, cut into 1 inch (2.5 cm) lengths and use lower 1/3 portion only
- 1 T sugar
- 1/4 c fresh cilantro, cut into small pieces

fresh or dried Thai chili peppers (optional)

- 1/4 t red curry paste and oil for garnish

1. Remove shells from prawns and rinse prawns and shells. Place shells in a pot with the 4 c water. Bring to a boil. Strain stock and discard shells.

2. Add prawns and mushrooms. Bring to a boil and stir. Combine sauce ingredients and add to soup stock. Heat through. Garnish soup with cilantro, chili peppers and curry paste.

ต้มข่าไก่

CHICKEN GALANGA COCONUT SOUP TOM KHA GAI

A very rich and creamy soup with the flavor of galanga.

⟨INGREDIENTS: 4 servings⟩

14 oz. (400g) coconut milk
½ lb. (225g) chicken breast, sliced
5 sliced dried galanga (kha)
1 T chopped lemon grass
5 kaffir lime leaves

3 T fish sauce
3 T lime juice
1 T sugar

½ c sliced mushrooms
cilantro and chili peppers for garnish

1. Combine coconut milk, chicken, galanga, lemon grass and lime leaves. Cook until chicken is almost done.

2. Add fish sauce, lime juice, sugar and mushrooms. Return to a boil and serve hot. Garnish with cilantro.

แกงไก่

RED CURRY CHICKEN

GANG GAI

Serve with Jasmine rice.

〈INGREDIENTS: 4 servings〉

14 oz.	(400g) can coconut milk
1 T	red curry paste
1/4 c	fish sauce
2 T	sugar
1 lb.	(450g) chicken breast, cut into inch pieces
5-8	kaffir lime leaves
1/4 c	fresh basil leaves

1. Combine 7 oz. (200g) coconut milk with curry paste.

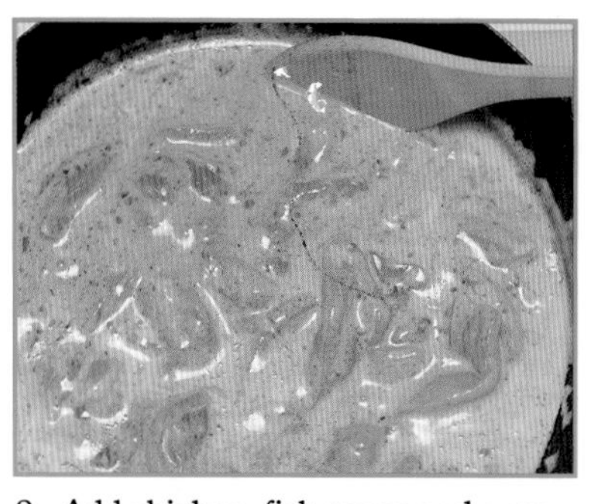

2. Add chicken, fish sauce and sugar. Bring to a gentle boil and cook until chicken is done.

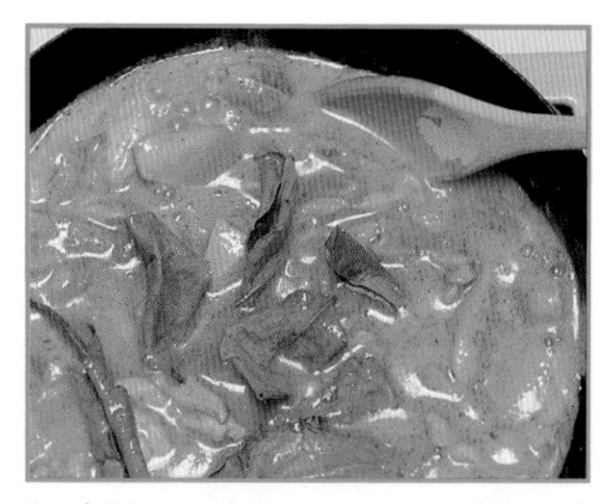

3. Add remaining coconut milk and lime leaves. Heat through. Garnish with basil just before serving.

แกงเขียวหวานไก่

GREEN CURRY WITH CHICKEN EGGPLANT AND BAMBOO

GANG KIEW WAN GAI

Serve with yellow rice.

〈INGREDIENTS: 4 servings〉

$^{1}/_{2}$ lb. (225g) chicken sliced

SAUCE:
6 T green curry paste (pg 17)
14 oz. (400g) coconut milk
$^{1}/_{4}$ c fish sauce
3 T sugar

$^{1}/_{2}$ c sliced egg plant
$^{1}/_{8}$ c slivered bamboo shoots

6 kaffir lime leaves

$^{1}/_{4}$ c basil leaves

red chili pepper for garnish

1. Combine chicken with sauce ingredients and bring to a slow boil. Continue to simmer until chicken is done. (approx. 8 minutes).

2. Add egg plant, bamboo shoots and lime leaves. Cook until egg plant is tender (approx. 3 mins.). Garnish with basil leaves and chili pepper before serving.

แกงมัสหมั่นเนื้อ

MUSSAMUN STEAK

MUSSAMUN NUEA

A favorite Thai Moslem recipe.

〈INGREDIENTS: 4 servings〉

- 1 lb. (450g) round steak
- 1 clove garlic, minced
- 2 14 oz. (400g) cans coconut milk
- 8 T Mussamun curry paste (See page 39)
- 6 T fish sauce
- 3 T sugar

- 2 T oil
- 1/8 c whole peeled peanuts

Optional: *Heat oil in frying pan and fry sliced onions, garlic and sliced red chili peppers for added color and flavor. Blend in a processor and add at the same time as the peanuts.*

1. Cut beef in cubes.

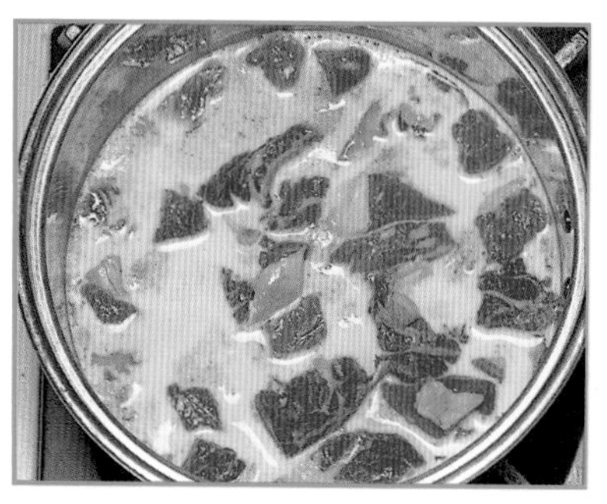

2. Combine beef with garlic and 14 oz. (400g) of coconut milk and simmer for 1/2 hour to tenderize the meat. Heat skillet, add oil and fry peanuts until golden brown. Remove and set aside.

3. Combine remaining 14 oz. (400g) coconut milk, mussamun curry paste, fish sauce and sugar. Add beef mixture and fried peanuts. Bring to a boil and cook for 5 minutes.

พะแนงเนื้อ

SAUTE BEEF CURRY

PA-NANG NUEA

This is a popular Thai dish, try chicken in this recipe.

〈INGREDIENTS: 4 servings〉

1 T oil

1/2 lb. (225g) sliced tender beef

Sauce:

5 T coconut cream
1 1/2 T red curry paste
2 T fish sauce
2 T sugar
5 kaffir lime leaves (soaked in water if dry)

1/8 c each sliced green and red bell peppers
1/4 c sliced onion
2 T ground roasted peanuts

Garnishes:

1/8 c coconut cream
5 kaffir lime leaves (soak in water if dry) sliced very thin

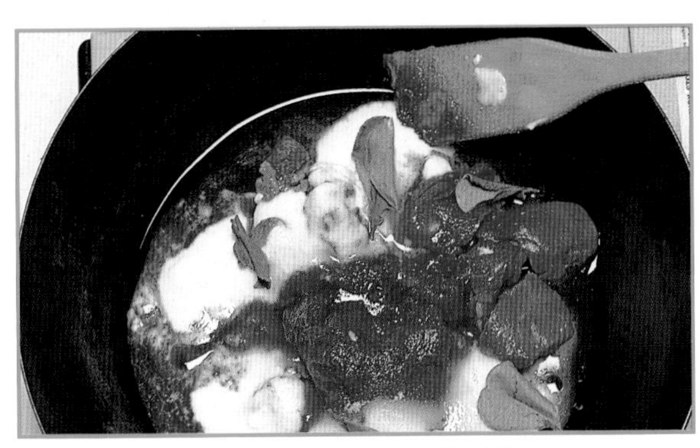

1. Heat pan and add oil. Saute beef adding sauce ingredients. Cook and reduce sauce until thick.

2. Add sliced peppers, sliced onion and ground peanuts. Cook for 2 minutes. Top mixture with garnish ingredients.

ไก่สะเต๊ะ

CHICKEN SATAY (MARINATED BEEF OR CHICKEN ON SKEWERS)

A favorite food sold by many street vendors in Thailand.

〈INGREDIENTS: 4 servings〉

1 lb. (450g) chicken breasts, sliced lengthwise 1 inch (2.5cm) wide (16 strips)

Marinade:

- 1/3 c coconut cream (thicker portion that floats to the top of a can of coconut milk)
- 1 t ground coriander seed*
- 3 T sugar
- 1 T yellow curry powder
- 6 T fish sauce
- 1 T oil

Garnishes: Cucumber, green leaf lettuce and sliced tomato

1. Thinly slice chicken breast.

2. In a large bowl mix all ingredients for marinade.

3. Dip each piece of chicken in the sauce and set aside. Cover and set in refrigerator for 15 minutes.

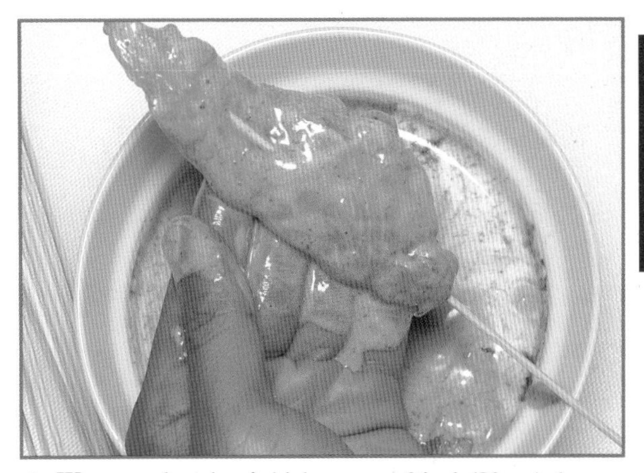

4. Weave each strip of chicken on an 8 inch (20 cm) skewer lengthwise.

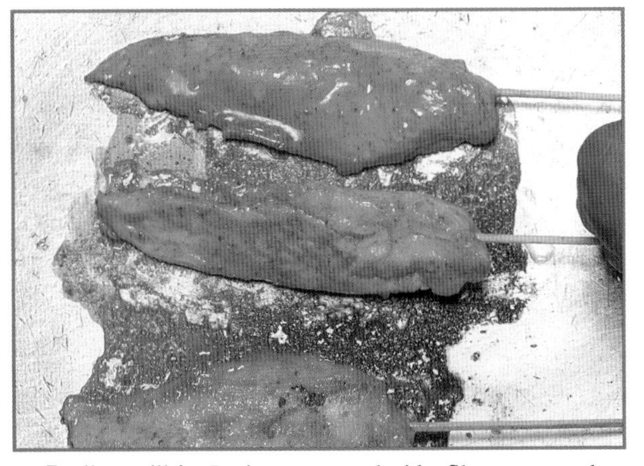

5. Broil or grill for 5 minutes on each side. Skewers can also be pan fried. To pan fry, brush a non-stick pan with coconut milk or left-over marinade and pan fry chicken 2-3 minutes each side, turn over and brush chicken with sauce.

NOTE:

Marinade can be used with beef. Slice 1 lb. (450 g) of top sirloin or flank steak into long narrow strips, 1 inch (2.5 cm) wide and 3 inch (8 cm) long. Proceed as with chicken.

Chopped fresh cilantro or Chinese parsley can be substituted for the ground coriander powder. Use approx. 2 T.

To grind your own coriander powder, take whole coriander seeds and saute lightly in pan until brown and aromatic. Grind in a blender or food processor until a coarse powder is formed.

เนื้อผัดผักคะน้า

BEEF WITH CHINESE BROCCOLI

NUEA PAD PUG KA NHA

A delicious one dish meal.

〈INGREDIENTS: 4 servings〉

- ½ lb. (225 g) Chinese broccoli
- ½ lb. (225 g) thin sliced beef

Marinade for beef:

- 2 cloves garlic, minced
- 1 egg
- 2 T sugar
- ⅛ t white pepper
- 1 t sesame seed oil
- 1 T rice wine
- 1 T cornstarch
- 2 T fish sauce

- 2 T oil

- ¼ c straw mushrooms
- 2 T oyster sauce

Garnish: Tomato roses

1. Clean broccoli and cut into 3 inch (8 cm) pieces and set aside. Combine beef with marinade.

2. Heat a skillet and add oil. Stir fry beef until almost cooked.

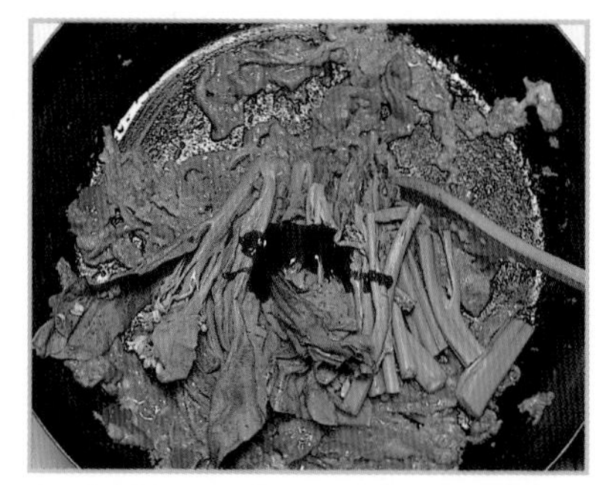

3. Add broccoli and remaining ingredients; continue to cook for approx. 3 more minutes.

ผัดใบกะเพรา

SPICY BASIL BEEF

PAD BAIGAPOA

A flavorful delicious served with rice.

〈INGREDIENTS: 4 servings〉

2 T	oil
4	cloves garlic, minced
1/2 lb.	(225 g) sliced tender beef
1 t	chopped Thai chilies, chopped
1/4 c	sliced onions
1 c	fresh basil leaves
1 T	oyster sauce
2 T	fish sauce
1 T	sugar
1/8 t	white pepper
1/4 c	chopped cilantro

1. Heat pan; add oil, garlic and chilies. Add beef and stir fry for 1 minute.

2. Add onions and basil. Cook for 1/2 minute, adding oyster sauce, fish sauce, sugar and white pepper. Top with green onions and cilantro.

ไก่ผัดขิง

GINGER CHICKEN

GAI PAD KEING

This is one of the most popular dishes in Thai restaurants.

⟨INGREDIENTS: 4 servings⟩

2 T oil	1/8 c slivered ginger root
1/2 lb. (225 g) boneless chicken breast, sliced	1/8 c sliced green pepper
2 cloves garlic, minced	1/8 c sliced red pepper
	1/8 c sliced mushrooms
	1/8 c sliced onions
2 T fish sauce	Optional garnish with cilantro
1 T oyster sauce	
1 T sugar	
pinch white pepper	

1. Heat pan, add oil, chicken and garlic. Cook for 2 minutes.

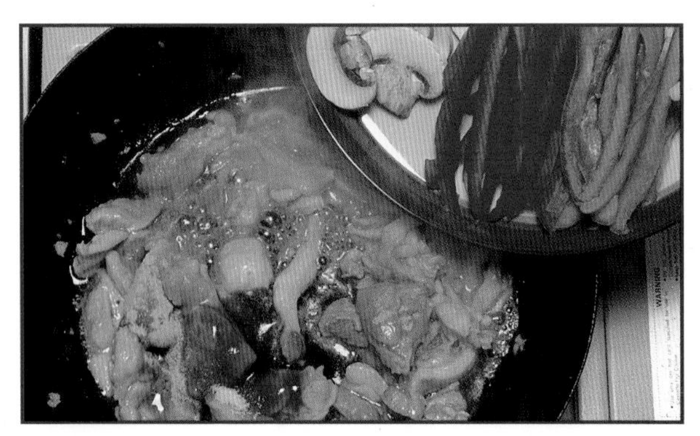

2. Add remaining ingredients and stir fry for 3 minutes more.

ผัดพริกเนื้อ

SPICY BEEF WITH KAFFIR LIME LEAVES PAD PRIG NUEA

Substitute dried kaffir lime leaves or fresh mint leaves if unable to find fresh kaffir lime leaves.

〈INGREDIENTS: 4 servings〉

- 2 T oil
- 3 cloves garlic, minced
- 5 Thai chili peppers or jalapeno peppers (chopped)
- 1 lb. (450g) beef, sliced thin against the grain
- 1/4 c sliced onions
- 1/4 c fresh kaffir lime leaves
- 1 c fresh basil leaves
- 2 T fish sauce
- 1 t seasoning sauce
- 1 T sugar
- 1/8 t white pepper
- 1 green onion, chopped
- 1/4 c chopped cilantro

1. Heat pan, add oil, garlic and chili peppers. Add beef and saute beef until almost done.

2. Add all vegetables and combine. Add fish sauce, seasoning sauce and sugar. Garnish with green onions and cilantro.

ซี่โครงหมูอบ

FIVE SPICE PORK SPARERIBS SEE KLONG MOO OB

Serve with fresh cucumber slices and whole sprigs of green onions.

⟨INGREDIENTS: 4 servings⟩

3 lbs. (1,350 g) pork spareribs

Marinade:

- 1/2 c soy sauce
- 1/4 c fish sauce
- 1 t five spice
- 1 T sesame seed oil
- 1/2 c sugar
- 3 cloves garlic, minced
- 1/4 c cilantro, minced
- 2 T rice wine or cognac
- 1 T oil

Garnishes: Parsley, radishes

1. Cut spareribs into 1 inch (2.5 cm) pieces.

2. Rub marinade into the ribs thoroughly and marinate for approx. 10 minutes.

3. Rub barbecue grill with oil. Place spareribs on grill. Barbecue for 10 minutes, bake in oven for 1/2 hour or broil for approx. 15 minutes.

พระรามลงสรง

RAMA CHICKEN (SWIMMING ANGEL) PARAMRONGSONG

Fried *tofu* is delicious instead of chicken.

〈INGREDIENTS: 4 servings〉

2 bunches spinach (blanch in water with oil to make spinach greener. Spread on serving plate.)

½ lb. (225 g) chicken breast sliced thin against the grain

7 oz. (200 g) coconut milk

2 T peanut sauce (Page 61)

Garnish: Ground roasted peanuts

1. Blanch spinach quickly in boiling water with a drop of oil. Remove to a platter and drain excess water.

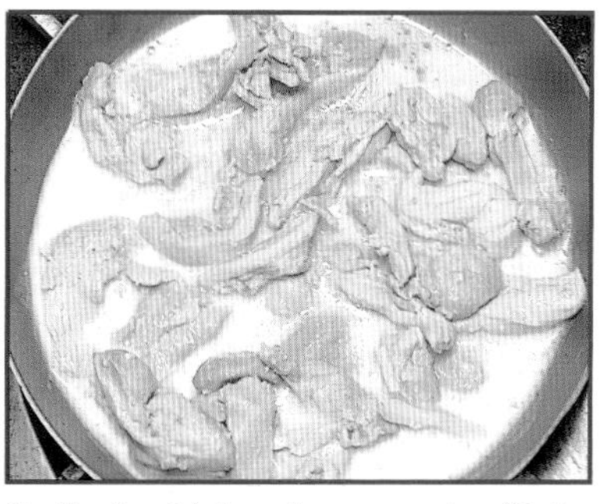

2. Cook chicken in coconut milk in frying pan until almost done. This will take approximately 10 minutes on medium heat.

3. Remove only chicken from pan and place on top of bed of blanched spinach. Pour peanut sauce over chicken before serving.

เนื้อสวรรค์

HEAVEN BEEF

Good recipe to serve with sticky rice or to take along on outings.

〈INGREDIENTS: 4 servings〉

3 lb. (1,350g) tender beef

Marinade:
3 T fish sauce
1 T soy sauce
1 t dry coriander
3 T sugar

2 c oil for frying

Garnishes: Green leaf lettuce, cucumber, tomato slices, green onion and cilantro

1. Slice beef into thin slices.

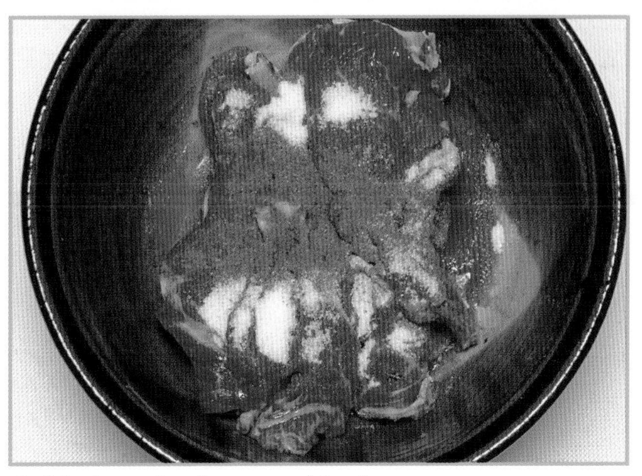

2. Marinate beef approx. 10 minutes.

3. Heat pan and cover with a thin coating of oil. Pan fry until sauce is reduced.

4. Deep fry beef on medium heat until beef floats to the surface. Fry in small batches at a time.

MUSSAMUN CURRY PASTE

5 T	oil
4	whole dried long red chili peppers
1/2 c	chopped onions
1/2 c	garlic cloves, chopped
1 T	chopped lemon grass
2	slices galanga
2	shallots
1/4 t	kaffir lime skin
2 T	dried coriander powder
1 T	cumin powder
1 t	cinnamon powder
1 T	star anise powder

1. Heat a saute pan and add 5 T oil on medium heat. Fry chili peppers, onions and garlic until golden brown.

2. Combine fried ingredients and all remaining ingredients in a blender and process until smooth. Store in a jar for future use.

ผัดเนื้ออยุธยา

AYUTTAYA BEEF

PAD NUEA AYUTTAYA

Serve with steamed white rice.

〈INGREDIENTS: 4 servings〉

- 2 T oil
- 2 cloves garlic, minced
- $1/4$ c minced onions
- $1/4$ c minced green bell peppers
- $1/4$ c minced red bell peppers
- $1/2$ lb. (225 g) beef, sliced thin against the grain

- 1 T oyster sauce
- 1 T sugar
- 3 T fish sauce

- $1/4$ c sliced red bell pepper
- $1/4$ c sliced green bell pepper
- $1/4$ c sliced mushrooms
- $1/4$ c slivered bamboo shoots
- $1/4$ c sliced onions
- $1/4$ c fresh basil leaves

Garnishes: Thai chili pepper and green onion

1. Heat pan. Add oil, garlic, minced onions and bell peppers. Add beef and stir fry for 1 minute. Add oyster sauce, sugar and fish sauce.

2. Add remaining ingredients and continue cooking for 3 minutes until vegetables are crisp tender.

เนื้อผัดถั่วฝักยาว

BEEF WITH STRING BEANS

NUEA PAD TUA FUG YOA

Other meats can be used.

⟨INGREDIENTS: 4 servings⟩

- 2 T oil
- 1 clove garlic, minced

- 1/2 lb. (225 g) lean ground beef
- 2 c string beans cut into 1 inch (2.5 cm) pieces
- 3 T fish sauce
- 1 t seasoning sauce
- 1 T sugar
- 1/4 c sliced green bell peppers
- 1/4 c sliced red bell peppers
- 1/4 t white pepper

- hot peppers (optional)

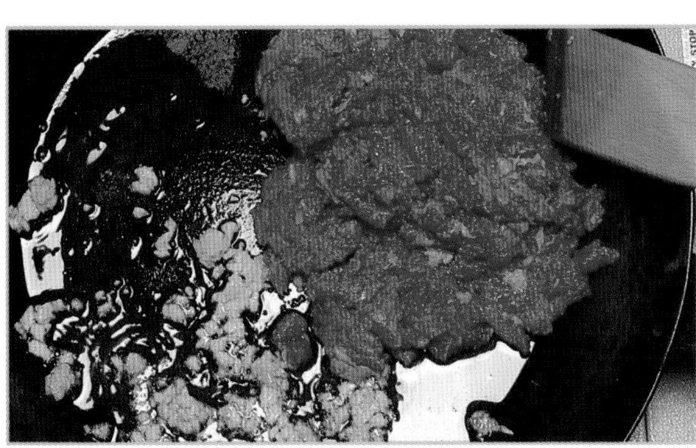

1. Heat pan; add oil and garlic. Saute ground beef until done on medium high heat.

2. Add beans and remaining ingredients and continue to cook until beans are tender.

ไก่ย่าง

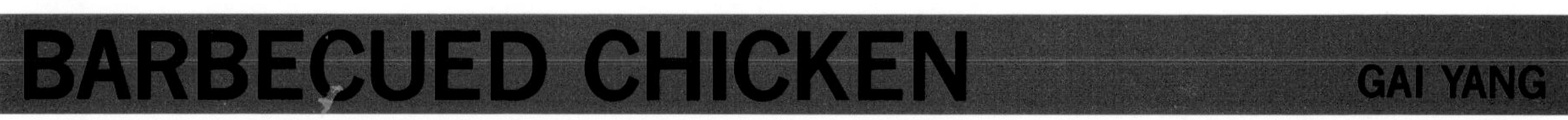

BARBECUED CHICKEN

GAI YANG

A good picnic recipe.

〈INGREDIENTS: 4 servings〉

1 whole chicken (approx. 3 lbs. (1,350g)) cut in half

Marinade:

- 1 t salt
- 1 T yellow curry powder
- 4 cloves garlic, chopped
- 1 t white pepper
- 1 T minced cilantro
- 2 T cognac or whiskey or rice wine
- 2 T coconut cream
- 1 T fish sauce
- 1 t ginger

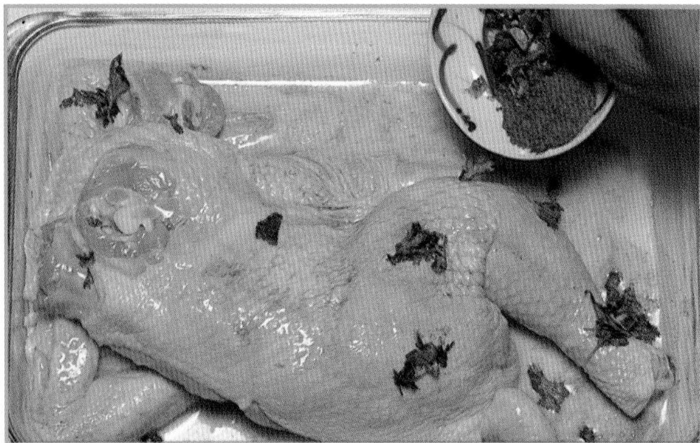

1. Rub entire chicken with marinade ingredients. Allow to marinate for 15 minutes.

2. Bake at 350°F (175°C) for 45 minutes and then broil for 10 minutes or until done.

3. Cut into serving size pieces and garnish before serving.

NOTE:

Serve with Chef Rut Royal Sauce (See page 69)

ไก่อบสุราษฎร์

BAKED LEMON GRASS CHICKEN GAI OB SU RATCH

Chicken can be served cut up or whole.

〈INGREDIENTS: 4 servings〉

1 whole chicken (approx. 3 lbs. (1,350g))

Marinade:

- 3 cloves garlic, minced
- 1/8 t white pepper
- 1/4 c fish sauce
- 2 T cognac or whiskey or wine
- 2 T chopped lemon grass
- 3 T coconut cream
- 1 T red curry paste
- 1 t salt

Garnishes: Slivered ginger root, broccoli, carrot, red cabbage and Royal Sauce

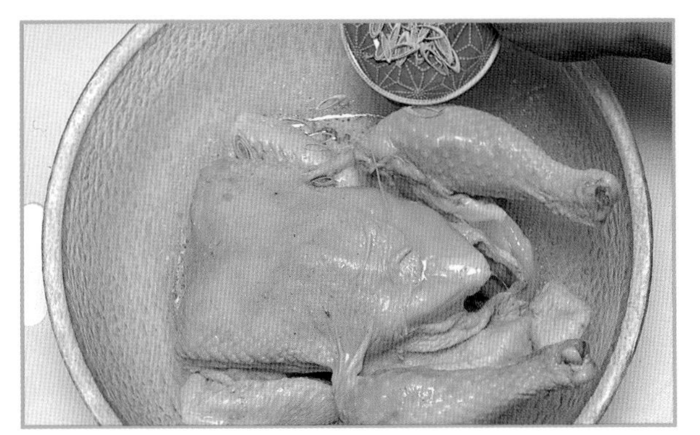

1. Thoroughly combine chicken with marinade and allow to set for 15 minutes.

2. Preheat oven to 325°F (163°C). Bake chicken for 1 hour or until done.

3. Serve chicken Thai style with Royal Sauce as a dip.

NOTE:
South of Thailand style baked chicken.

ไก่ผัดผัก

VEGETABLES WITH CHICKEN
GAI PAD PUG

A delicious one dish complete meal.

〈INGREDIENTS: 4 servings〉

- 2 T oil
- 2 cloves garlic, minced

- 1 c thin sliced chicken breast
- 1/4 c sliced onions
- 1/2 c sliced carrots
- 1 c sliced cabbage
- 1 c broccoli flowerets
- 1/2 c sliced cauliflower
- 1/2 c each sliced red and green bell pepper
- 1/4 c snow peas
- 1/4 c sliced mushrooms
- 1/4 c beansprouts

Sauce:

- 1 T fish sauce
- 1 T oyster sauce
- 1 T sugar

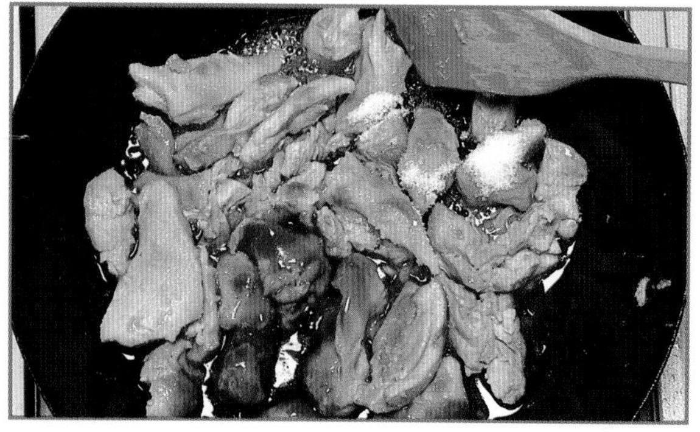

1. Heat a frying pan and add oil and garlic. Stir fry chicken until done.

2. Add all vegetables and sauce ingredients. Stir fry for 4 minutes until vegetables are crisp tender. Serve hot with steamed white rice.

เนื้อผัดพริก

PEPPER STEAK

NUEA PAD PRIG

Delicious served over steamed Jasmine rice with fried egg.

〈INGREDIENTS: 4 servings〉

2 T oil

1/2 lb. (225 g) beef sliced

Marinade:
1 T burgundy wine
1 t fish sauce
1 t cornstarch
1/4 t white pepper
4 cloves garlic

1/8 c sliced onions
1/4 c sliced green bell peppers
2 T fish sauce
1 t seasoning sauce

1 T sugar
1 t sesame seed oil
Garnishes: Fresh basil leaves and Thai chili pepper

1. Combine beef with marinade.

2. Heat pan, add oil and saute beef with garlic, onions and peppers for 3 minutes, add remaining ingredients and continue cooking for 2 minutes.

เสือร้องไห้

TIGER CRY STEAK

SERUA RONG HI

This a favorite Northern style recipe.

〈INGREDIENTS: 4 servings〉

1 lb.(225g) tender beef steaks
(1 inch, 2.5cm in thickness)

Marinade:
2 T fish sauce
1 T soy sauce
1 T chopped cilantro
1 stalk chopped lemon grass

Garnishes:
Green leaf lettuce, sliced cucumbers, sliced tomatoes, fresh pea pods, cabbage, mint and basil leaves, green onions, cilantro, carrots, green bell pepper and red bell pepper

Serve with dipping sauce:
3 cloves garlic, minced fine
2 T fish sauce
3 T lime juice
1 t hot pepper

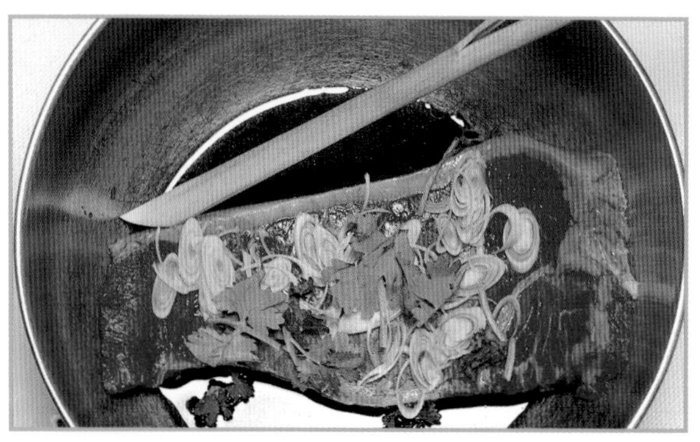

1. Marinate the beef 3 minutes per side.

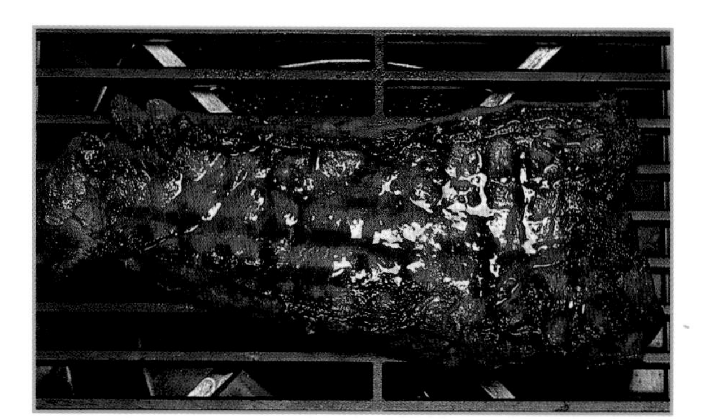

2. Broil approx. 4 minutes per side. Slice thin against the grain. Garnish with sliced vegetables and place the sliced beef on top.

หมูย่างตะไคร้

LEMON GRASS PORK CHOPS MOO YANG DA KAI

Serve with royal sauce as a dip.

〈INGREDIENTS: 4 servings〉

1 lb. (450g) pork chops

Marinade:

3 cloves garlic, minced
1/8 t white pepper
2 T fish sauce
1 T soy sauce
1 T sesame seed oil
1 T cognac or whiskey or wine
2 T chopped lemon grass
1 T green onion
3 T coconut cream
1 t sugar

Optional garnishes: Yellow bell pepper, sliced tomatoes and lettuce

1. Make marinade.

2. Thoroughly combine pork chops with marinade, allow to set for 10 minutes.

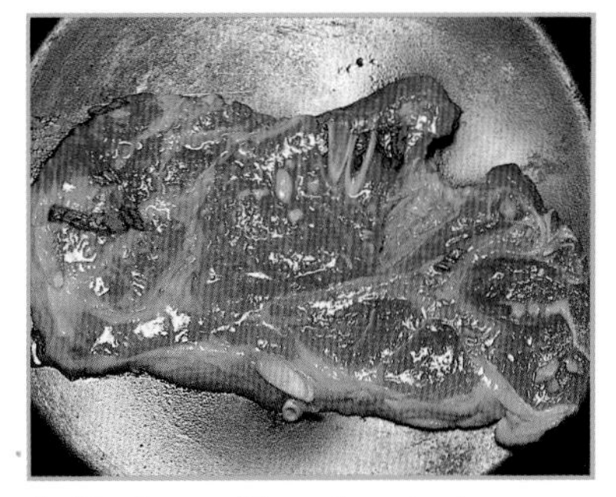

3. Broil or grill until pork chops are done, turning once. (Approx. 8 minutes per side.)

ไก่ผัดถั่วหิมพานต์

CASHEW CHICKEN
GAI PAD MAMUANG HIM MA PAHN

A favorite dish on the Restaurant menu.

〈INGREDIENTS: 4 servings〉

- $\frac{1}{4}$ T oil
- 2 cloves garlic, minced
- $\frac{1}{2}$ lb. (225 g) sliced chicken

Sauce:

- 1 T fish sauce
- 2 T oyster sauce
- $1\frac{1}{2}$ T sugar
- 1 t sesame seed oil
- $\frac{1}{8}$ t white pepper

- $\frac{1}{2}$ c roasted cashew nuts
- 1 green onion, chopped
- $\frac{1}{8}$ c sliced red bell pepper

1. Heat pan, add oil, garlic, chicken and all sauce ingredients.

2. Turn heat to high and reduce sauce until a glaze forms. Mix in roasted cashews, garnish with green onions and bell peppers.

แกงคั่วสับปะรด

PINEAPPLE CURRY WITH SHRIMP GANG KUA SUBPAROD

Serve with Jasmine rice. Also good with mussels or smoked salmon.

〈INGREDIENTS: 4 servings〉

14 oz. (400g) coconut milk
1 c crushed canned pineapple
2 T red curry paste
$^1/_4$ c fish sauce
$1^1/_2$ T sugar
2 T lemon juice

$^1/_2$ lb. (225g) shrimp, shelled and deveined

Garnish: Fresh lime leaves

1. Combine all ingredients except shrimp and bring to a boil.

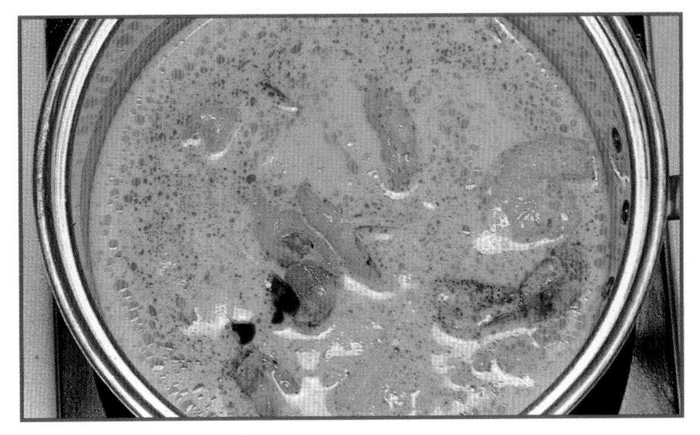

2. Add shrimp and cook until done.

WHOLE FISH WITH GARLIC SAUCE

Delicious served with chicken curry.

〈INGREDIENTS: 4 servings〉

1 whole fish (approx. 1 lb. (450g)) cleaned
1 T rice wine (*sake*)
1/2 c all purpose flour

4 c oil for deep frying

SAUCE:
Blend together:
6 cloves garlic
1/4 c green bell pepper
1/4 c red bell pepper
1/4 c onion
1/8 c cilantro

3 T oil
1/4 c fish sauce
2 T sugar

1/4 c sweet basil leaves
Garnish: Red cabbage

1. Cut 3 slashes to the bone on both sides of the fish. Sprinkle with rice wine.

2. Flour fish on all sides.

3. Heat oil to 350°F (175°C) and carefully immerse fish into the hot oil.

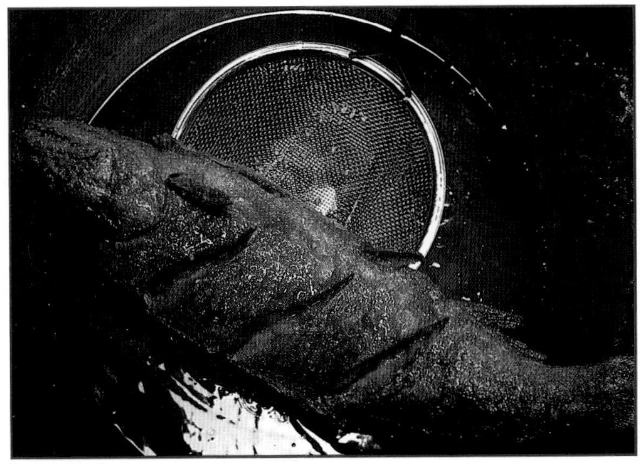

4. Deep fry fish until done, turning once. (Approx. 6 minutes each side.)

5. Blend together garlic, bell peppers, onion, cilantro and white pepper to a coarse consistency. Set aside.
Heat a skillet, add oil. Add blended mixture and all other ingredients. Cook mixture for approx. 5 minutes on medium high heat. Add basil and combine. Remove fish and pour sauce over fish. Serve with nam pla prig pg 69.

RED CURRY PASTE

Paste ingredients

1/2 c	chopped onions
8	cloves garlic
10	dried chilies (dried red chili peppers)
4	slices fresh galanga (or 1/4 t laos powder)
2 T	chopped lemon grass
1 T	chopped coriander root or stems
1/2 t	cumin
1 t	shrimp paste
1 t	salt
3 T	oil

1. Combine all ingredients in a blender and process until smooth.

2. Heat a frying pan on medium high heat; add 3 T oil. Slowly fry curry paste ingredients for 5 minutes until it is fragrant. Remove and store in a jar for future use.

ปลานึ่งบ้านไร่

STEAMED WHOLE FISH COUNTRY STYLE PLA NUNG BAAN RAI

Serve with favorite dipping sauce.

⟨INGREDIENTS: 4 servings⟩

1	whole fish (snapper or rock cod approx. 2 lbs. (900g))
1 T	oil
2 T	rice wine
1/2 t	salt
1/2 t	white pepper
3 T	fish sauce
3 T	lime juice
2	stalks lemon grass, smashed and cut in large pieces
1/4 c	sliced onions
2	garlics, smashed
2	green onions, smashed
4	Thai chili peppers, fresh or dried, smashed
1 T	slivered ginger root
1/4 c	basil leaves

Garnishes: Cilantro, lemon slices, green leaf lettuce

1. Slash whole fish on both sides.

2. Place fish on a steaming plate. Spread remaining ingredients evenly on top of entire fish. Steam for 25 minutes. Serve.

ฉู่ฉี่ปลา

STEAMED CURRY FISH

CHOO CHEE PLA

Boneless fish fillets can be used.

〈INGREDIENTS: 4 servings〉

1 whole fish (approx. 1 lb. (450g))
1 T oil
2 T red curry

Sauce:
14 oz. (400g) coconut milk
3 T fish sauce
2 T sugar
5 kaffir lime leaves

Green and red bell pepper slices for garnish kaffir lime leaves for garnish

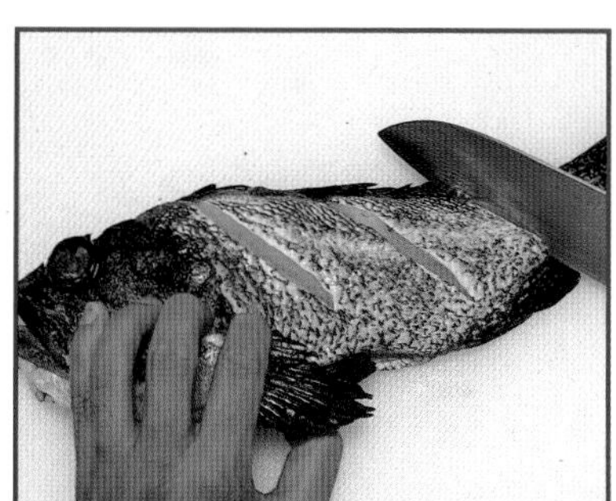

1. Clean fish and cut 3 slashes to the bone on both sides. Heat frying pan and add oil, stir fry curry 1/2 minute on medium heat.

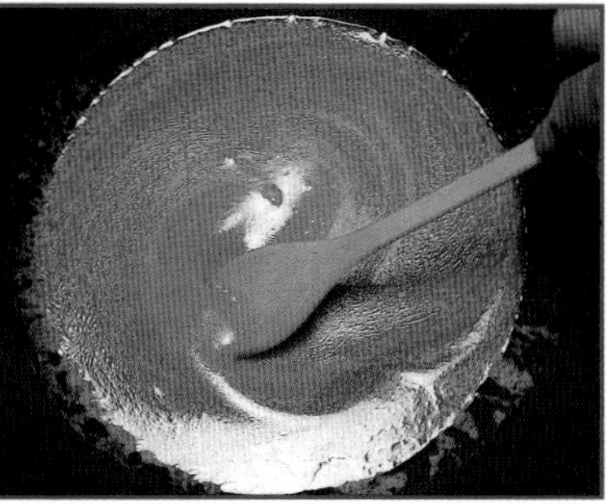

2. Combine remaining sauce ingredients.

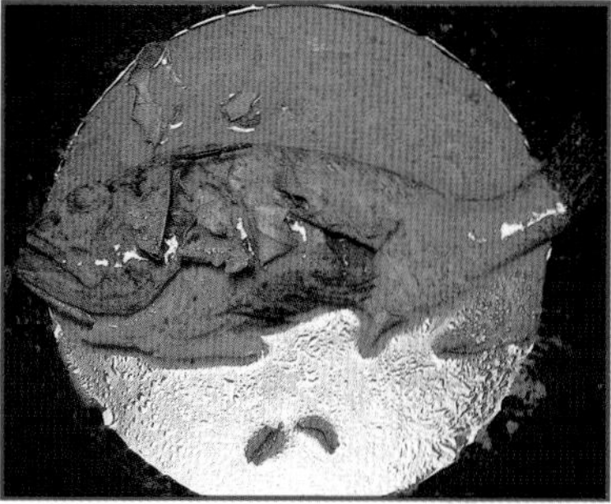

3. Carefully place fish in pan and bring to a slow boil. Cover, bring sauce to a slow boil. Ladle sauce over fish during cooking. Simmer approx. 20 minutes.

ผัดทะเล

SEAFOOD COMBINATION

PAD TALAY

Delicious recipe for any fish fillet.

⟨INGREDIENTS: 4 servings⟩

- 2 T oil
- 2 cloves garlic, chopped
- 6 prawns, shelled and de-veined
- $\frac{1}{2}$ c scallops
- 3 oz. (85g) snapper fillets, cut into 1 inch (2.5cm) slices
- 6 fresh clams (cleaned of sand)

- $\frac{1}{4}$ c sliced red pepper
- $\frac{1}{4}$ c sliced green pepper
- $\frac{1}{2}$ c sliced onions
- $\frac{1}{4}$ c sliced bamboo shoots
- $\frac{1}{4}$ c sliced fresh mushrooms

SAUCE:

- 3 T fish sauce
- 2 T sugar
- 1 T oyster sauce
- $\frac{1}{2}$ t white pepper

cilantro for garnish

1. Heat pan, add 2 T oil and garlic. Add all seafood, stir fry for $\frac{1}{2}$ minute.

2. Add all vegetables and sauce ingredients. Cover, cook 4 minutes on medium heat. Garnish with cilantro and serve.

ผัดโป๊ะแตก

LEMON GRASS SEAFOOD COMBINATION PAD PO TAK

Good accompanied with yellow rice.

⟨INGREDIENTS: 4 servings⟩

2 T oil

1/4 lb. (115 g) shrimp, shelled, deveined
1/8 lb. (56 g) scallops
1/4 lb. (115 g) fish, sliced 1/2 inch (1.5 cm) thick
1/4 lb. (115 g) mussels, cleaned

3 T green curry paste
3 T coconut creme

3 T fish sauce
1 1/2 T sugar

1/8 c slivered bamboo shoots
1 stalk lemon grass cut into 1 inch (2.5 cm) lengths
1/4 c sliced red pepper
1/4 c sliced green bell pepper
1/4 c basil leaves

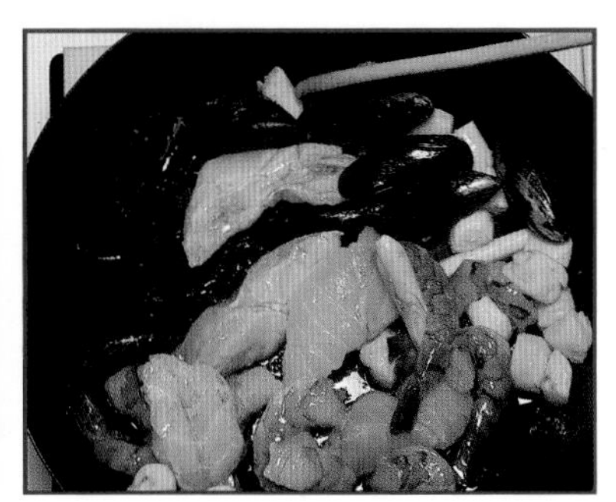

1. Heat pan and add oil. Add all seafood and saute for 1 minute.

2. Add vegetables and gently combine.

3. Add seasoning ingredinets. Cover pan and continue cooking for approx. 3 minutes.

ห่อหมก

SALMON WRAPPED IN BANANA LEAF

Serve with hot steamed white rice.

〈INGREDIENTS: 4 servings〉

1 lb. (450g) salmon, skinless, boneless, cut into large chunks

Sauce:

- 1/4 c red curry paste
- 1 c coconut creme
- 2 egg yolks
- 2 T fish sauce
- 2 T cornstarch
- 1 c lettuce
- 1 c zucchini, sliced

- 1 large banana leaf, cut into 6 (8 × 8 inch) pieces
- 1 c holy basil leaves

Garnish: Cilantro

1. Marinate salmon chunks with sauce and place in refrigerator to chill for approx. 15 minutes.

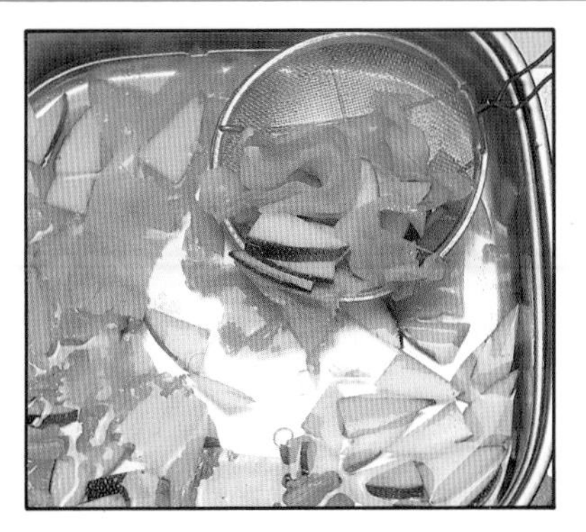

2. Blanch lettuce and zucchini and set aside.

3. Wipe each piece of banana leaf with damp cloth before use. Place 1/4 portion of blanched vegetables and salmon in center of each piece of banana leaf. Top with a scattering of basil leaves.

4. To close packet, bring sides together.

5. Fold in ends.

6. Use a small piece of wood resembling a tooth pick to close packet.

7. Arrange packets in a steamer and steam for 15 minutes or until done. Packets can also be baked in oven at 350°F (175°C) for approx. 20 minutes.

ปูผัดผงกะหรี่

STIR FRIED CRAB WITH CURRY

POO PAD PONG GA-RHEE

Serve with a salad or favorite vegetable dish.

〈INGREDIENTS: 4 servings〉

1	whole crab
2 T	oil
1 T	crushed garlic
1 c	sliced onions
1/8 c	sliced mushrooms
1/8 t	white pepper
2 T	rice wine
2 T	fish sauce
2 T	sugar
1 T	oyster sauce
1/4 t	white pepper
1	green onion, sliced
1/4 c	cilantro
1	egg

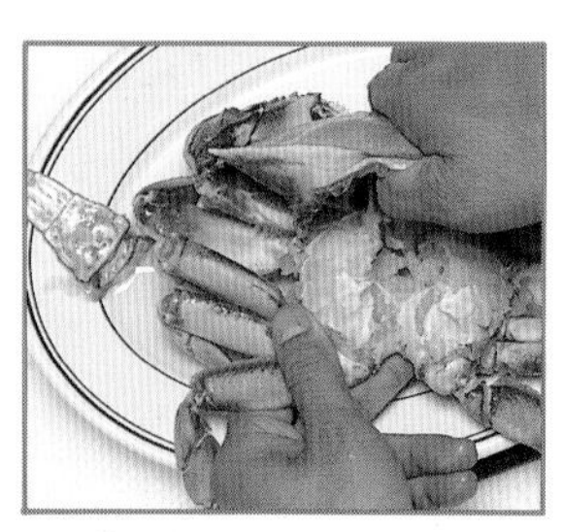

1. Clean crab.

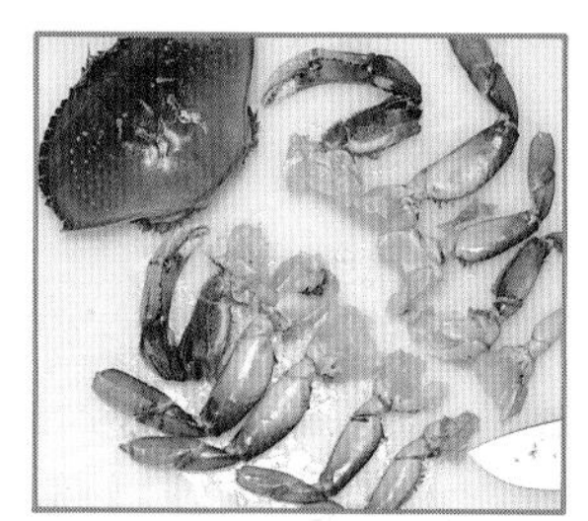

2. Separate and crack crab.

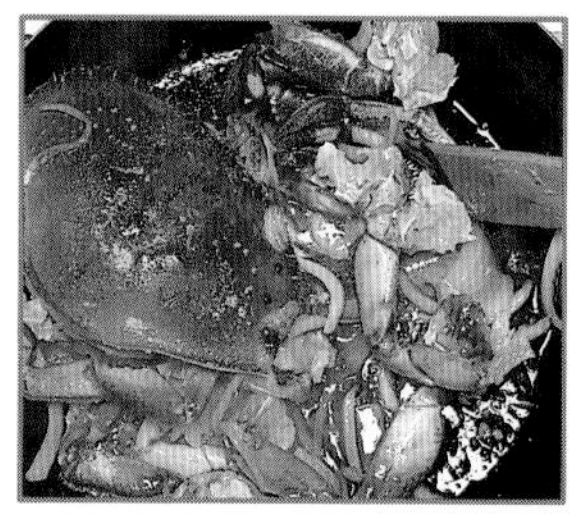

3. Heat pan; add oil, garlic, crab, onions, fish sauce, sugar and oyster sauce. Cover and steam contents for 5 minutes.

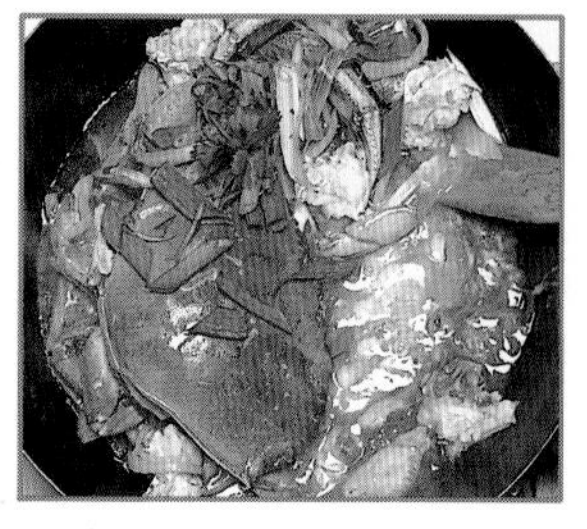

4. Add green onions, cilantro and stir in egg. Continue cooking until egg is cooked. Serve with lemon wedges.

ผัดเผ็ดหอย

SAUTÉED CLAMS WITH BASIL PAD PED HOY

Mussels are a delicious alternative to clams or use a combination of both.

〈INGREDIENTS: 4 servings〉

2 T oil
1 t red curry paste
1 lb. (450g) clams
2 T fish sauce
2 t sugar
1/8 c sliced green bell pepper
1/8 c sliced red bell pepper
1 T slivered fresh ginger root
1/4 c basil leaf

Garnish: Green leaf lettuce

1. Heat pan, add oil, curry paste and saute clams for 1 minute.

2. Add fish sauce and sugar.

3. Add peppers, ginger and basil; cover pan and cook for 3 minutes on medium heat.

ทอดมัน

THAI FISH CAKE

Serve with Royal Sauce.

〈INGREDIENTS: 4 servings〉

½ lb. (225g) salmon fillet
3 T Grand Palace Red Curry Paste
2 T fish sauce
1 egg
3 T cornstarch
¼ t baking soda

6 kaffir lime leaves, sliced very thin (or use basil leaves)

3 c oil for deep frying (325°F, 163°C)

Garnishes: Green leaf lettuce, cucumber, sliced tomatoes

1. Remove all bones from fish and slice the meat. Combine with remaining ingredients in a food processor.

2. After the mixture is thoroughly combined, continue to whip mixture or throw the mixture against the side of the bowl, adding lime leaves. Use water to wet hands while throwing mixture against side of bowl.

3. Shape into 2 × 1 inch (5 × 2.5 cm) thick patties. Set aside on tray until ready to fry.

4. Deep fry at 325°F (163°C) until light golden brown.

NOTE: *Use string beans as an option. When using dried kaffir lime leaves, soak until soft before using.*

PEANUT SAUCE

1	14 ounce (400 g) can coconut milk
2 T	red curry paste
1/4 c	fish sauce
3 T	sugar
1 c	ground roast peanuts

Combine all ingredients in a sauce pan and simmer for 15 minutes stirring constantly.

GARLIC SQUID

PLA MUG TOD GATIEM PRIG THAI

A favorite dish at lemon Grass Grill Restaurant.

〈INGREDIENTS: 4 servings〉

½ lb. (225 g) cleaned squid

Marinade:

5	cloves garlic, minced
2 T	white wine
⅛ t	white pepper
1 T	cornstarch
2 T	fish sauce
1 T	soy sauce
1 T	sugar

2 T oil

Garnishes:
Green leaf lettuce, cucumber, carrot, tomato slices and cilantro.

1. Slash the mantel of squid diagonally. Then cut diagonal slashes in the opposite direction. Slice into 2 inch (5 cm) pieces.

2. Combine squid with marinade ingredients.

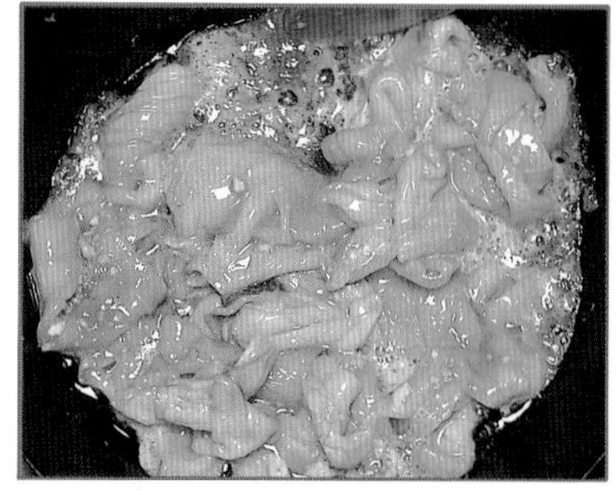

3. Heat the pan; add cooking oil and saute squid on medium high heat until all the squid curls. Garnish and serve.

PATTAYA SHRIMP

GOONG PAD PONG GAHEE

Serve with Jasmine rice.

⟨INGREDIENTS: 4 servings⟩

1/2 lb.	(225 g) shrimp, shelled and deveined
2 T	oil
2	cloves garlic, minced
1 t	curry powder
2 T	fish sauce
1 T	oyster sauce
1 1/2 T	sugar
1/4 c	slivered green bell pepper
1/4 c	slivered red bell pepper
1/4 c	sliced mushrooms
1/4 c	sweet basil leaves
1/4 c	sliced onion

1. Heat pan; add oil, garlic and shrimp. Saute 1 minute. Add all seasoning ingredients.

2. Add all vegetables and cook for 2 minutes.

เส้นหมี่ลาดหน้าหมู

MAIFUN WITH CREME SAUCE

A variety of other noodles can be used.

〈INGREDIENTS: 4 servings〉

1/2 lb. (225g) pork loin, sliced thin

Marinade for pork:
1 T cornstarch
1 egg
2 t sesame seed oil
1/2 t white pepper
1 T seasoning sauce

2 T oil
1/2 lb. (225g) maifun
2 T sweet soy sauce

2 T oil
1 T crushed garlic
1 c water

3 T fish sauce
2 T sugar

2 T cornstarch dissolved in small amount of water

1 c broccoli flowerets
1/2 c sliced carrots
1/4 c sliced red peppers
1/2 c fresh pea pods
1/4 c straw mushrooms
1 green onion, cut into 1 inch (2.5cm) length

Garnish: Cilantro

1. Marinate pork for 10 minutes.

2. Soak noodles in warm water until soft. (Approx. 10 minutes)

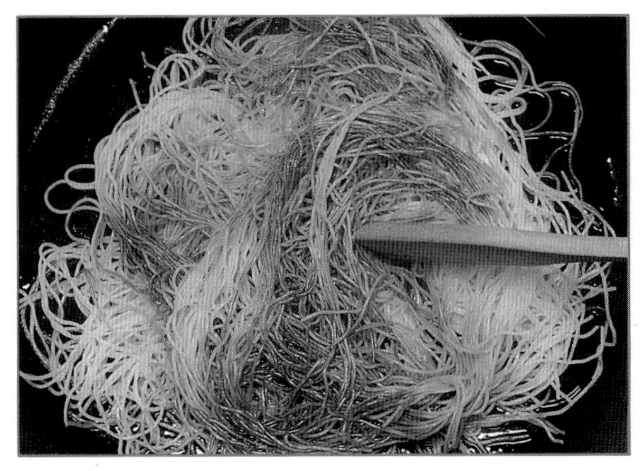

3. Heat pan, add 2 T oil and stir fry noodles adding sweet soy sauce. Throughly mix. Remove and set aside.

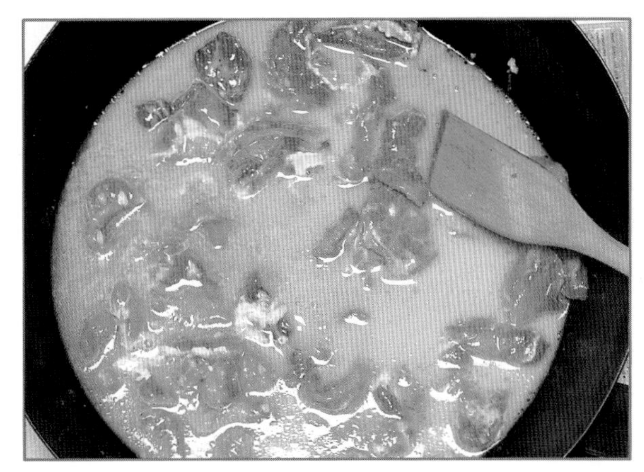

4. Heat pan, add 2 more T oil, garlic, water, fish sauce and sugar. Add pork and bring mixture to a boil. Add enough cornstarch mixture to form a medium thick sauce.

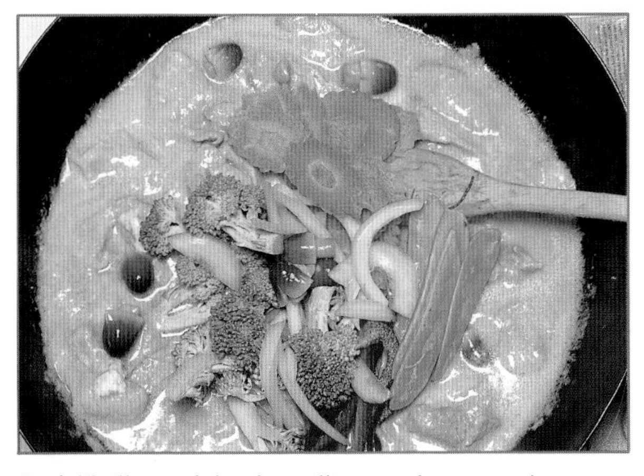

5. Add all remaining ingredients and return mixture to a boil cooking for 3 more minutes. Pour mixture over noodles and serve.

ผัดซีอิ๊ว

STREET NOODLES

PAD SEI EW

A popular lunch dish in Bangkok.

1/2 lb.(225 g) beef, sliced thin

Marinade for beef:
- 1 clove garlic, minced
- 1 egg
- 1 T cornstarch
- 1 T rice wine
- 1 T fish sauce
- 1 T oyster sauce
- 1 T sugar
- 1 t sesame seed oil
- 1/2 t white pepper

2 T oil

1/2 lb. (225 g) fresh rice noodles

- 1 T fish sauce
- 1 T sugar
- 1 T oyster sauce
- 1 T sweet soy sauce

- 1 c broccoli flowerets
- 1/8 c sliced carrots

Garnishes: Cilantro, green onion and tomato slices

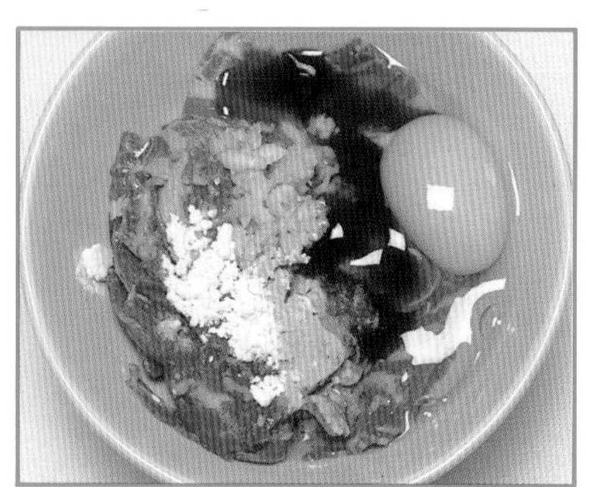

1. Combine beef with marinade for 10 minutes.

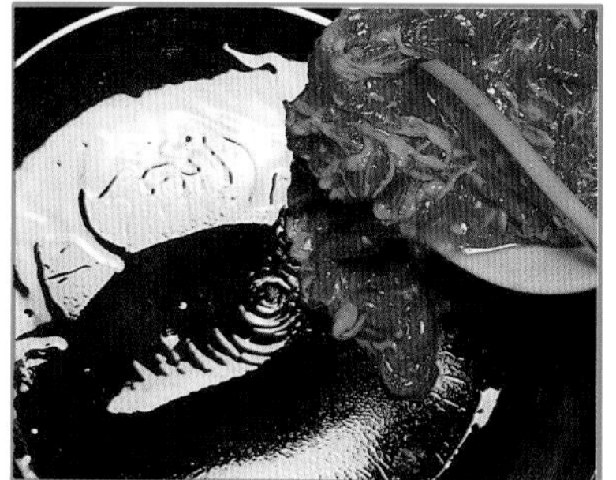

2. Heat pan, add oil. Stir fry beef until done.

3. Add noodles and all remaining ingredients. Continue to cook until sauce is reduce and all ingredients are hot.

หมี่กรอบ

CRISPY NOODLES

MEE GROB

Serve as a first course.

〈INGREDIENTS: 4 servings〉

6 oz. (170g) maifun (rice sticks)
4 c oil (375°F (190°C))

Sauce:
1/2 c vinegar
1/2 c sugar
1 t salt
1 t tomato paste

2 eggs (optional for garnish)
1/4 c chopped green onions
1/4 c chopped red bell pepper

2 T chopped cilantro

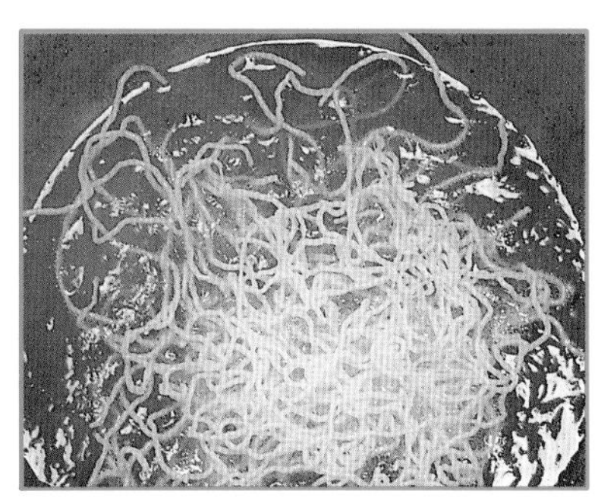

1. Fry rice sticks in hot oil until puffed, remove and set aside.

2. While oil is still hot, beat eggs and fry eggs in streams and remove.

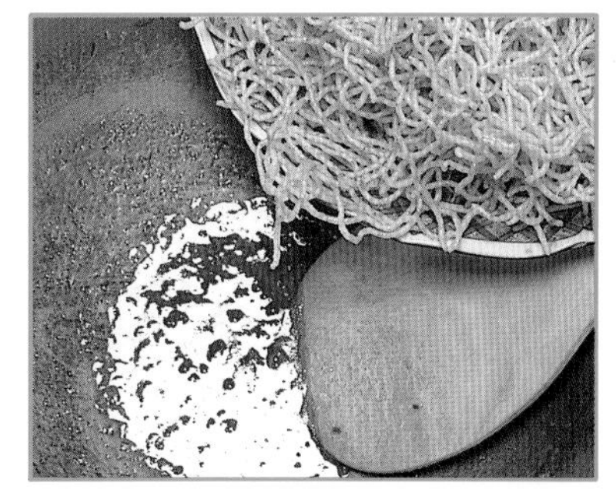

3. Combine sauce in a frying pan or wok and reduce to a syrupy stage. Add noodles to pan and mix with sauce. Mix quickly so noodles are evenly coated with sauce. Place on serving dish and garnish with chopped green onions, red pepper and eggs.

ผัดไทย

THAI NOODLES

Other ingredients may be added such as fried *tofu*, chicken and preserved vegetables.

⟨INGREDIENTS: 4 servings⟩

8 oz.	(225 g) dried rice noodles
3 T	oil
1	clove garlic, minced
1	egg
1/4 lb.	(115 g) shrimp, shelled and de-veined
1/4 c	water (use only as needed if noodle mixture is too dry)
1/4 c	fish sauce
1/4 c	sugar
1 T	paprika
1	green onion, cut into 1 inch (2.5 cm) lengths
1/4 c	ground roasted peanuts
1 c	beansprouts

Optional garnishes:
Cilantro, lime slices

1/2 c each of bean sprouts, shredded carrots, red cabbage and lemon slices.

1. Soak rice noodles in cold water for 2-3 hours or until soft.

2. Heat frying pan until hot; add garlic and egg and shrimp. Scramble until done. Reduce temperature to medium if necessary.

3. Drain noodles and add to mixture in pan. Stir fry until translucent, adding a small amount of water if required.

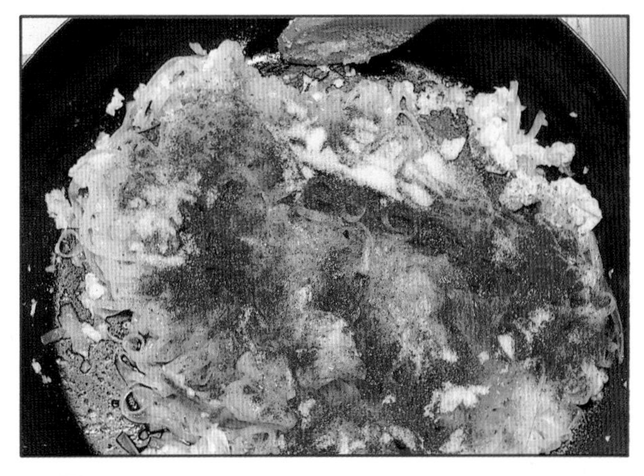

4. When noodles are soft, add fish sauce, sugar and paprika. Throughly combine and reduce sauce.

5. Mix in peanuts, bean sprouts and green onions. Garnish and serve.

THAI DIPPING SAUCES

NAM PLA PRIG

1/4 c fish sauce
5 T lemon or lime juice
2 cloves garlic, minced
5 whole THAI chili peppers, chopped (PRIG KEE NOO)

Combine all ingredients and use as a dipping sauce. Also can be used in curries or stir fried dishes.

PRIG DONG

6 Whole jalapeno chili peppers, sliced
1/3 c vinegar

Combine peppers with vinegar and use as a sauce or dip for noodles or other dishes to improve or change the flavor.

ก๋วยเตี๋ยวแขก

CURRY NOODLE

A noodle dish with Moslem influence.

〈INGREDIENTS: 4 servings〉

- 1 lb. (450g) rice noodles or wheat noodles, cooked and rinsed.

- 1 lb. (450g) beef, cut into 1 inch (2.5cm) cubes
- 2 cans coconut milk
- 1/2 c fish sauce
- 3 T sugar
- 1 c water
- 2 T curry powder

- 1/2 c bean sprouts, blanched
- 1/2 c swamp cabbage or spinach
- 1/2 c Chinese broccoli
- 1/4 c ground toasted peanuts
- 3 T lime juice
- 2 T sugar
- 1/4 c oil
- 1/4 c minced onions
- 2 T minced garlic

Garnishes: Cilantro, green onion and red bell pepper

1. Cut beef in 1 inch (2.5 cm) cubes.

2. Simmer beef in 1 can of coconut milk until beef is tender (approx. 45 minutes).

3. Add second can of coconut milk, fish sauce, sugar, water and curry powder to the beef mixture. Cook for 5 minutes.

4. Bring a pot of water to a boil. Add noodles and all other ingredients; remove to a serving dish.

5. Top noodles with soup mixture.

Optional: Fry minced onions and garlic separately in skielet until golden brown. Serve with noodles.

STEAMED RICE

3 c Jasmine rice
3 c water

1. Place rice in a sauce pan. Rinse twice to clean rice. Drain water from rice thoroughly. Add water.

2. Cover sauce pan and bring to a boil and allow to boil on high heat for 1 minute. Turn temperature to low and steam for 10 minutes. Reduce temperature to lowest setting and allow to steam for 10 minutes more. Serve hot.

NOTE: *An electric rice cooker can be used following the same proportions of rice to water.*

ข้าวผัดปู

CRAB FRIED RICE

KHOW PAD POO

A delicious accompaniment for any dish.

〈INGREDIENTS: 4 servings〉

1 T butter
1 clove garlic, chopped
1/2 c cooked crab meat
1 egg

2 c cooked rice
1 T seasoning sauce
1 T fish sauce
1 T sugar

1/4 finely diced yellow bell pepper
1 green onion, chopped

Garnishes:
1 tomato, sliced
1/2 c sliced cucumber
cilantro

Sauce:
2 T fish sauce
2 T lemon juice
fresh Thai chili peppers

1. Heat frying pan and add butter. Stir fry garlic, crab.

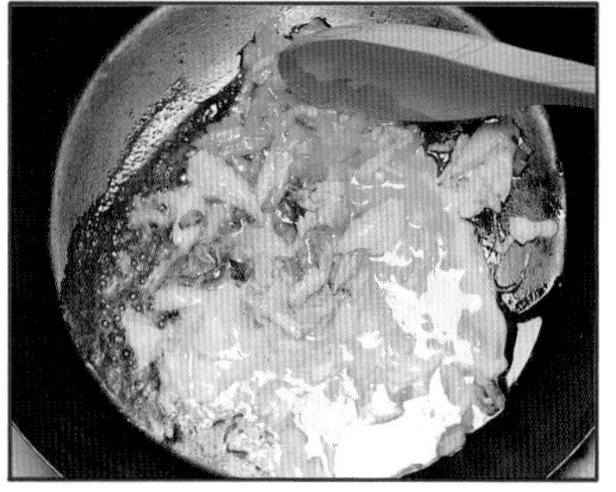

2. Add egg together until done.

3. Add rice, seasoning sauce, fish sauce and sugar. Continue to stir fry until rice mixture is hot. Add yellow peppers and green onions. Garnish with remaining ingredients and serve with sauce on the side.

ข้าวผัดหมู

PORK FRIED RICE

KHOW PAD MOO

An easy dish as a complete meal.

〈INGREDIENTS: 4 servings〉

2 T oil
1 clove, garlic minced
1/2 c sliced pork

1 egg
2 c cooked white rice

2 T fish sauce
1 T sweet soy sauce
1 T sugar
1/4 t white pepper

1/2 c sliced onions
1/8 c sliced red peppers
1/8 c sliced green peppers
1/2 c tomato chunks

1 green onion, chopped

Garnishes:
cilantro
cucumber slices

Sauce:
2 T fish sauce
Thai chili peppers
2 T lemon juice

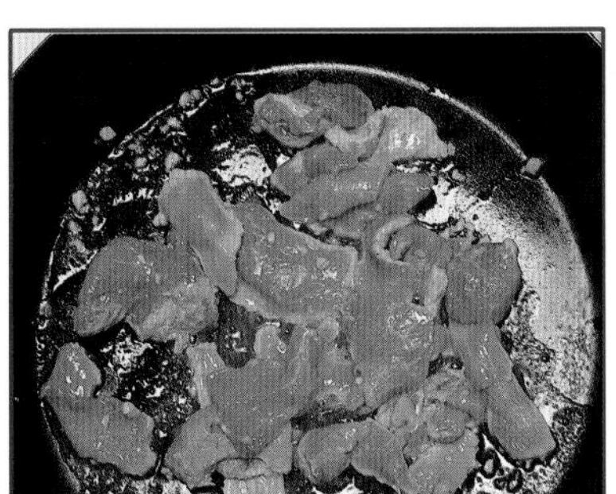

1. Heat frying pan, add oil and garlic. Stir fry pork until done.

2. Add egg and scramble until cooked. Add rice, soy sauce, fish sauce, sugar and white pepper. Continue cooking until rice is hot reducing temperature if necessary.

3. Add onions, sliced peppers and tomato chunks. Toss in green onions. Garnish with cilantro and cucumber slices. Serve with sauce.

ข้าวอบสับปะรด

BAKED RICE IN PINEAPPLE WITH CASHEW NUTS KHOW OB SUBPAROD

This mixture can also be wrapped in banana leaf and baked 350°F (175°C) for 15 minutes or until hot.

〈INGREDIENTS: 4 servings〉

1 whole fresh pineapple (cut in half lengthwise)

2 T oil
1/2 lb. (225 g) diced chicken

Seasoning:
1/4 c fish sauce
1 T seasoning sauce
1/4 c sugar
1/3 c coconut milk
1/4 t white pepper

1/2 c toasted cashew nuts
1/2 c crushed pineapple
1/4 c raisins
2 T chopped cilantro
3 c cooked Jasmine rice

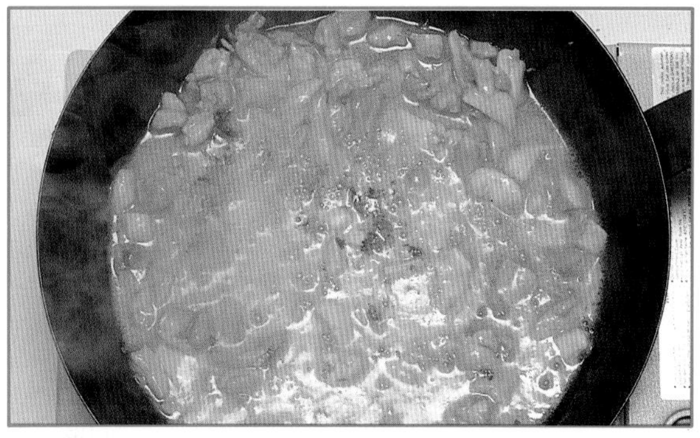

1. Cut pineapple in half lengthwise and remove meat of fruit so pineapple can be used as a container. Heat a frying pan and add oil. Cook chicken until done. Add all seasonings and allow mixture to cook until mixture foams.

2. Add cashews, pineapple, raisins, chopped cilanatro and rice. Turn off heat and thoroughly mix. Stuff rice into pineapple and bake in a 350°F (175°C) oven for 20 minutes or until hot. (Can microwave for 5 minutes instead of baking in oven).

SQUASH DESSERT

GANG BOUT FUG THONG

A delicious Thai dessert.

〈INGREDIENTS: 4 servings〉

½ pumpkin
1 14 oz. (400g) can coconut milk
1 can coconut sugar

1. Peel squash and slice thin.

2. Bring coconut milk to a boil adding ¼ c coconut sugar. Stir and bring to a boil.

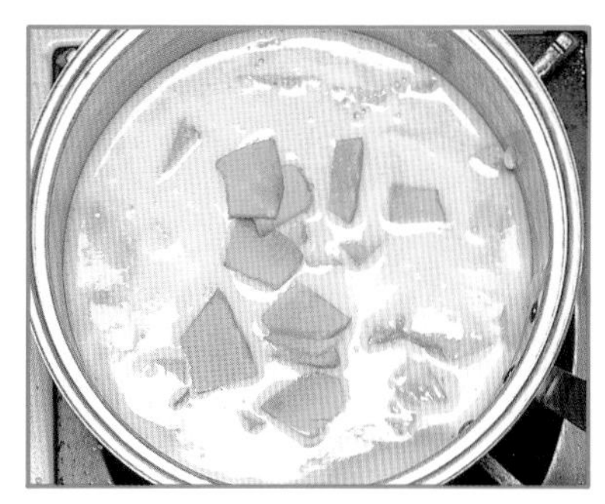

3. Add sliced squash and simmer for 15 minutes.

ชาเย็น

THAI ICED TEA

CHA YEN

A refreshing cold drink.

〈INGREDIENTS: 4 servings〉

1/2 c Thai tea leaves
5 c water

6 T sweetened condensed milk
1/4 c evaporated milk
ice cubes

Garnish: Mint leaves

1. Pour sweetened condensed milk and evaporated milk into glass.

2. Brew Thai tea leaves with water. Use coffee maker for easier brewing.

3. Combine strained brewed Thai tea with sweetened condensed milk and evaporated milk. Allow mixture to cool.

4. Pour over ice cubes and top with additional evaporated milk.

กาแฟเย็น

THAI ICED COFFEE

CAFE YEN

Good as an after dinner drink or summer drink.

⟨INGREDIENTS: 4 servings⟩

1/4 c instant coffee
2 c hot water

1/4 c sweetened condensed milk
1/4 c evaporated milk

ice cubes

1. Dissolve instant coffee in hot water.

2. Combine coffee with sweetened condensed milk and evaporated milk.

3. Pour mixture into glasses filled with ice and top with additional evaporated milk if desired.

สาคูเปียก

TAPIOCA PUDDING

SAKOO PAIK

Pudding may be served warm. Toasted sesame seeds can be sprinkled on top of pudding.

⟨INGREDIENTS: 4 servings⟩

1 c small tapioca pearls
4 c water

1/2 c sugar
1/2 c coconut creme
1 1/2 c assorted canned Thai fruits, sliced (Jack fruit, longan, lychee, coconut meat, rambutan, palm seed)

Topping:
1/2 c coconut creme
1/4 c sugar
1/2 t salt

1. Rinse tapioca pearls; add water. Bring to a boil, stirring constantly. Reduce to simmer and cook for 15 minutes or until all pearls are soft and clear. Add sugar and coconut creme.

2. Stir in sliced fruits and some of the syrup as desired for a thinner consistency.

ข้าวเหนียวดำ

BLACK RICE PUDDING

KHOW NEO DOM

The black rice has a firm texture served with coconut creme.

⟨INGREDIENTS: 4 servings⟩

1 c black rice
6 c water
1/2 c sugar
1 8 oz. (225g) can coconut milk

Topping:
1/2 c coconut creme
1/2 t salt
1/4 sugar

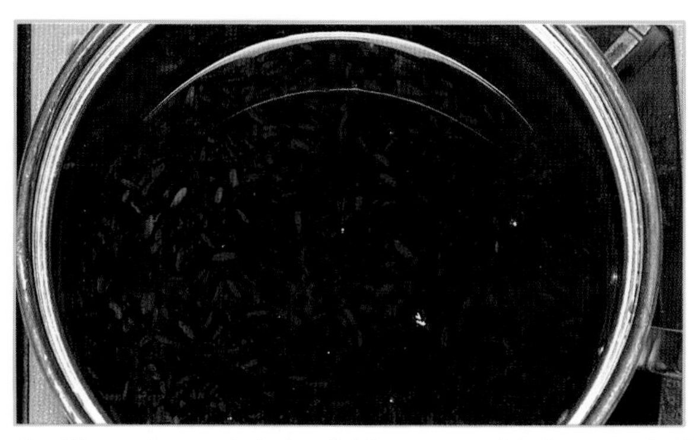

1. Rinse rice and drain. Add water and bring to a boil; reduce temperature to a slow simmer and cook for 45 minutes or until rice is soft.

2. Add sugar and coconut milk; stir well and simmer for 10 minutes more. Combine topping ingredients. Pour a small amount over each serving of rice pudding.

สังขยา

THAI CUSTARD

SUNKAYA

A traditional Thai dessert. Can be served with Thai sweet rice.

〈INGREDIENTS: 4 servings〉

6 eggs
1 c coconut creme
1 c sugar
1/2 t Jasmine flavor extract

Optional garnish: Cooked egg yolk

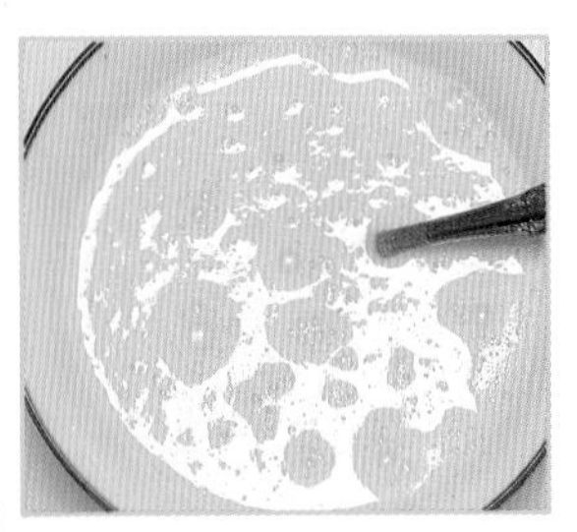

1. Combine eggs, coconut creme.

2. Add sugar and Jasmine extract. Beat together for 2 minutes.

3. Heat a 9 inch (23 cm) round cake pan in a steamer. Pour egg mixture into cake pan; cover steamer and steam for approx. 1/2 hour.

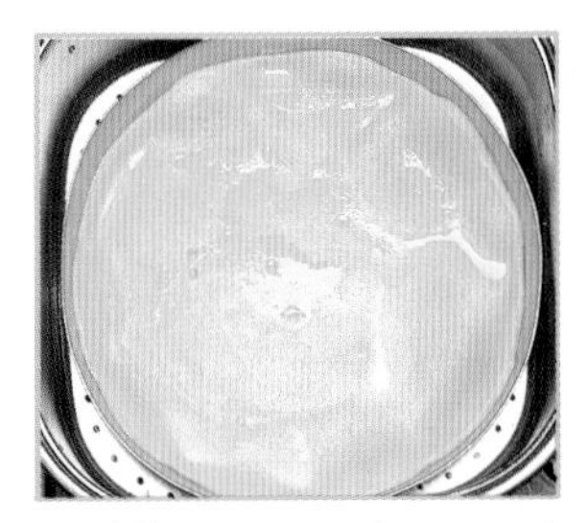

4. Allow custard to cool and cut into 12 equal pieces.

INFORMATION

EQUIPMENT

Very few pieces of equipment are required for the cooking of Thai food. Most kitchens of today are supplied with the essentials such as knives, a cutting board, sauce pans, skillets and other cooking utensils. To accomplish the desired results, equipment can be improvised or substitutions made for other special items found in a typical Thai kitchen.

A very essential piece of equipment in a traditional Thai kitchen is the mortar and pestle. This consists of a deep ceramic or stone bowl to contain the ingredients needed in the making of curry pastes or other dips and sauces. The stone or wooden pestle, shaped like a rod, is used to pound, mash or crush the ingredients. This is accomplished by the rhythmic pounding of the spices, herbs and other seasonings until the desired consistency is achieved. A blender or food processor can be used instead of a mortar and pestle.

The wok, a round-bottom, curved pan, makes the cooking of some of the recipes much easier and is specially suited for the method of deep frying. Compared with a deep fryer, a wok requires less oil for deep frying and also allows for the quick stir-frying of some Thai dishes—due to the shape of the wok. If a wok is not available, a deep pan can be substituted as a deep fryer and a good skillet can be used to achieve the stir fry action necessary for the combining of stir fried recipes.

Strainers, used in the cooking of other cuisines, are practical pieces of equipment required in the fast removal of noodles or other foods from soups or sauces. A good quality strainer is always helpful for any task requiring the removal of ingredients from deep frying oils, soups or soaking processes.

A good quality bamboo steamer consisting of several tiers can be purchased at an Asian grocery or supermarket. The steamer is placed atop a wok filled with boiling water, thus creating the steam required to cook certain recipes and desserts.

The convenience provided by the electric rice cooker has made the cooking of rice very quick and easy. Rice cooked by this method is always delicious and fluffy, eliminating the chores of adjusting the temperature and constantly monitoring the cooking time, which are called for in using a sauce pan to cook rice. Such a sauce pan should be of good quality, deep and used with a tight-fitting lid. Following the cooking instructions will result in properly cooked rice.

DINING THAI STYLE

Thai people share dishes as in family style meals. Most foods are already cut into bite-sized pieces, and each person takes only enough for one or two mouthfuls, allowing everyone to share the same dish. The table setting includes a fork and spoon. The fork is held in the left hand to assist in pushing the food onto the spoon, which is held in the right hand. To cut foods into smaller portions, the fork is used to hold the food in place while the spoon, held in the right hand, cuts the food.

All dishes arrive simultaneously. Selection from among the dishes on the table is left up to the individual's preferences. Dining Thai style means enjoying the company of everyone at the table as well as the flavorful tastes of each dish.

MENU PLANNING OF A THAI MEAL

A Thai meal consists of many courses and is a combination of dishes eaten family style. In planning a typical menu, consider flavors to entice the palate as well as the eye. Offer different dishes comprised of sweet, sour, savory and hot or spicy flavors.

In preparing foods pleasing to the eye, consider the cutting techniques of all the foods as well as the texture of the foods. The cutting of vegetables and meats should be varied as the texture and tastes are dependent upon the size and shape of the food.

COOKING METHODS

In a traditional Thai meal, soup does not precede the other courses as in the Western style of meal service, but rather, soup is served as an accompaniment throughout the entire meal. Other dishes in the meal may include a salad, a stir-fry meat or vegetable dish along with perhaps a seafood dish. A plate of cut fresh fruit or a Thai dessert would be a good ending to the meal.

Basic Cutting Methods

When preparing ingredients use a sharp knife. Cut to bite size pieces making them easy to cook, and eat. For decorative cuts, use the tip of knife. For peeling use the lower part of blade. The part from the center towards the tip is used for most cutting work.

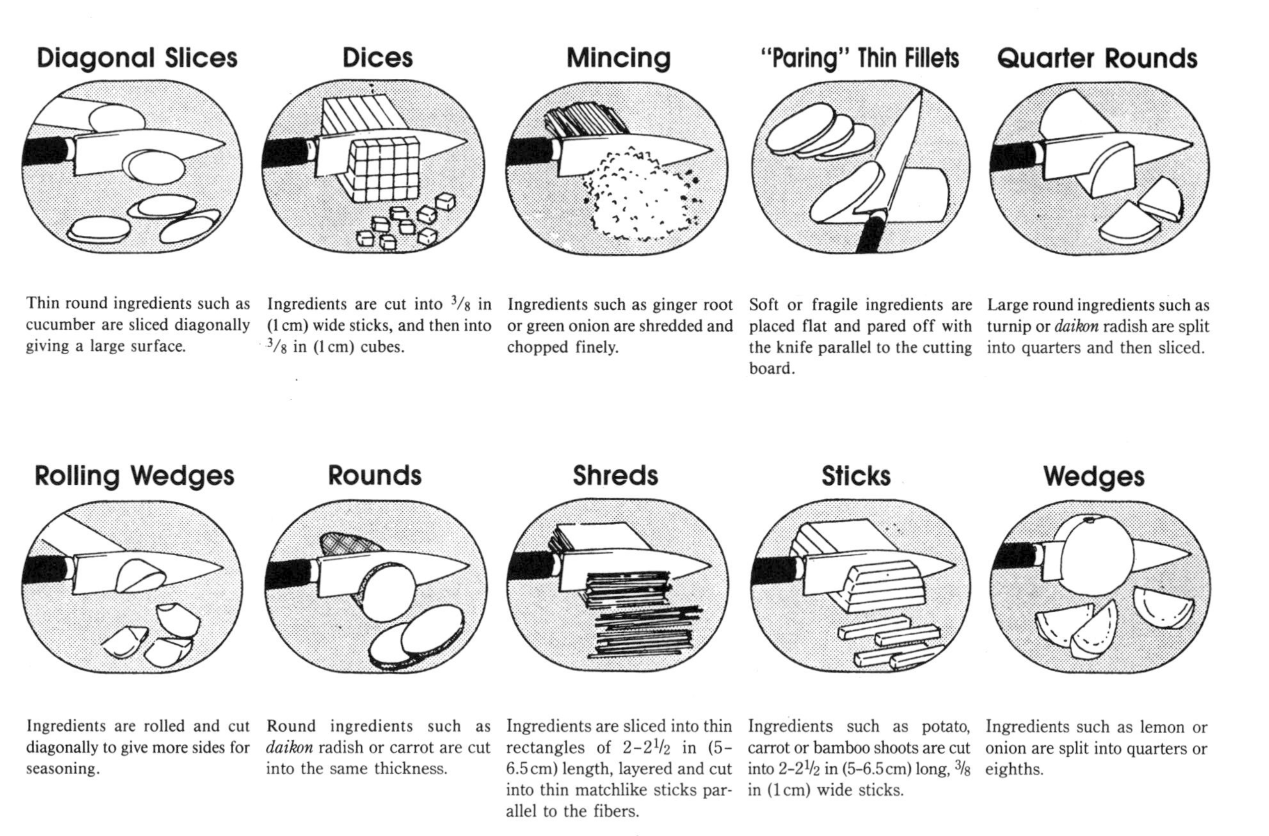

Diagonal Slices: Thin round ingredients such as cucumber are sliced diagonally giving a large surface.

Dices: Ingredients are cut into 3/8 in (1 cm) wide sticks, and then into 3/8 in (1 cm) cubes.

Mincing: Ingredients such as ginger root or green onion are shredded and chopped finely.

"Paring" Thin Fillets: Soft or fragile ingredients are placed flat and pared off with the knife parallel to the cutting board.

Quarter Rounds: Large round ingredients such as turnip or *daikon* radish are split into quarters and then sliced.

Rolling Wedges: Ingredients are rolled and cut diagonally to give more sides for seasoning.

Rounds: Round ingredients such as *daikon* radish or carrot are cut into the same thickness.

Shreds: Ingredients are sliced into thin rectangles of 2–2½ in (5–6.5 cm) length, layered and cut into thin matchlike sticks parallel to the fibers.

Sticks: Ingredients such as potato, carrot or bamboo shoots are cut into 2–2½ in (5–6.5 cm) long, 3/8 in (1 cm) wide sticks.

Wedges: Ingredients such as lemon or onion are split into quarters or eighths.

Deep-frying

Deep frying is used to prepare "batter-fried" foods.

Four points for successful DEEP FRYING

1) Fresh ingredients. 2) Good vegetable oil. 3) Constant frying temperature. 4) Smooth batter.

Prepare all ingredients to be deep-fried ahead of time. Preferably keep in a refrigerator until last minute. Make the batter just before the actual deep-frying. Then mix batter lightly.—All foods should be thoroughly dried before dredging. If you prefer a thick coating to thin batter, use less water than called for in the recipe.

In general, deep-frying requires a large amount of oil in the wok, heavy cast iron skillet or deep-fryer. The use of polyunsaturated vegetable oil is strongly recommended for deep-frying. None of the pure vegetable oils contains cholesterol. The right temperature for deep-frying is 330–355°F (165–180°C). The oil should reach this temperature before any ingredients are added. An easy way to tell whether the oil has reached the desired temperature is adding a drop of batter into the oil. If the drop of batter reaches the bottom and slowly returns to the surface, the oil is not yet hot enough. If the batter drops half way to the bottom and immediately bounces up to the surface, the oil is ready for deep-frying. Drop in ingredients and deep-fry until golden. Adjust the temperature to maintain a constant frying temperature. Frying temperature of 340°F (170°C) is recommended for vegetables. Use deep-frying thermometer to maintain a constant oil temperature. Skim the surface of the oil occasionally to keep it clean. Start with vegetables and then shrimp which requires a higher temperature. The oil used for deep-frying can be saved and reused. To grant your oil longer life, remove crumbs with a fine mesh strainer. The quality of used oil is judged by its clarity, not by the number of times used nor the length of time used. Fresh oil is light in color and clear. If the used oil is still relatively clear, it is readily useable again. For the second time around, it is recommended to deep-fry chicken or meats coated with bread crumbs. To remove odor in oil, deep-fry some potatoes uncoated. The moisture in potatoes absorbs odor while it is deep-fried. The proportion of 3 : 1 (used oil: fresh oil) is also useable again for deep-frying meats and chicken. To store the used oil, first strain with a fine mesh strainer while oil is still hot. Then place the oil in a heatproof container and allow to cool. Cover and store in dark and cool place or in the refrigerator.

Grilling, Broiling, Pan-frying, Baking, Barbecueing

The grilling method is used to cook food quickly over very high heat so that the outside is crisp while the inside flesh remains tender and moist. The ingredients must be fresh. Grilling can be done in two different ways: direct and indirect heat. If you do charcoal grill, prepare charcoal fire in advance so that the heat gets very hot. For stove top grilling, coat the rack with thin film of oil, then heat the unit before you place food on. Fish and meats are often marinated or basted with marinade sauces before and during cooking. Marinade sauces are combinations of wine or sugar, soy sauce and fresh ginger which has the same tenderizing enzyme as papaya and pineapple. Grill 60% on one side and 40% on the other side. For pan-frying, heat and add a small amount of oil. Heat the oil, then tilt the skillet so the oil covers the surface. When the oil begins to show a light haze, it is ready to pan-fry the ingredients. Cook over high heat, so that fish or meat except pork is tender and moist inside and the flavor is sealed in. If longer cooking is necessary, reduce heat and cover for a few minutes. You may need to add some marinade sauce to the pan. Then remove the lid and continue to cook until all liquid evaporates. For oven baking, preheat the oven to the required temperature and place food in the center of the oven to allow for even baking.

Steaming

Steaming is one of the best ways of retaining more nutrients and natural flavor than other conventional means of cooking. Steaming seals in the natural juices of meats and vegetables which are delicious when served over rice. There are many different types of steamers. A wok with a cover will work as a good steamer. Multi-tiered bamboo steamers may be purchased. However, a large pot with a cover will suffice for the purpose of steaming food. Steaming racks are necessary to support and elevate the plate or bowl which holds food steamed in a wok. A round cake rack will do just as well as commercially available steaming racks. You may improvise using water chestnut cans with both ends removed. The rack should be put in the center of the wok or pan. All steamers operate according to the same basic principle. The efficient circulation of steam is of paramount importance. Bamboo steamers have several tiers in which many dishes can be steamed simultaneously. The tiers and cover are set on top of a wok containing boiling water. There are also metal steamers consisting of a pot to hold the water, usually two tiers and a cover. For example, the bottom pot cooks soup stock while the two tiers are used to steam two other separate dishes. In this manner, many dishes may be steamed at once, saving time and energy.

Follow the steps below for effective steaming

1) Pour water into the wok or pot so that the water level stands 1 inch (2.5 cm) below the steaming rack or dish of food. 2) Cover the wok and bring the water to a full boil. 3) Use only heatproof dishes for steaming. 4) Place the dish of food atop the steaming rack. Cover and bring to the boiling point again. Turn the temperature down to medium high and allow to steam for the specified time. 5) Check the water level when longer steaming is necessary.

Stir frying, Sautéing

This cooking method combines the elements of high heat and constant tossing to seal in the flavor and juices of meat and vegetables. Thus, this technique is often used for Thai cooking. Stir-frying cooks protein foods thoroughly, at the same time leaving them tender and juicy. Vegetables retain their natural color and crisp texture when stir fried. It is important that slices are uniform in size so that they can be cooked evenly. Some vegetables may need parboiling before stir-frying. Prepare all necessary seasonings before stir-frying. Heat the wok or skillet until it barely gets hot and add a small amount of oil (usually 2 T), then roll the oil around to cover the surface of the wok. When the oil begins to show a light haze, add the ingredients. Follow the recipe and remember to adjust the temperature control at the proper stir-frying temperature. Actual stir-frying involves vigorous arm action in the constant stirring and tossing of the food. Serve immediately while still hot.

GLOSSARY

BAMBOO SHOOTS ··· The cone shape shoot of the bamboo plant. It is easiest to purchase the canned variety which comes whole or in slices or shreds. Once opened, bamboo shoots should be stored in a different container in fresh water in the refrigerator. Available at Asian grocery stores.

BANANA LEAVES ··· The large leaves of the banana tree. Used often times for lining plates, wrapping various foods for cooking to impart flavor. These leaves are usually sold in Asian grocery stores frozen. Wipe the leaves with a damp cloth before using. This is a very versatile material with many uses either for cooking or garnishing.

BASIL (SWEET) ··· A fresh sweet basil with dark green leaves with a purple stem. The flavor is that of aromatic licorice. Fresh mint can be an acceptable substitute in cooking.

BEAN CURD (*TOFU*) ··· The solid curd of soy bean milk. Fresh bean curd is sold packed in water. Keep in water in the refrigerator.

BEAN SPROUTS ··· The sprouts of the mung bean. Use fresh sprouts if possible. Store bean sprouts in fresh water and store in the refrigerator.

BLACK BEAN SAUCE ··· A combination of mashed fermented black beans with ginger and garlic. Now this mixture comes conveniently in jars. Keeps indefinitely.

BLACK MUSHROOMS ··· These mushrooms are usually sold dried. Soak the mushrooms only until soft and rinse. Remove stem and use as directed in recipe. These mushrooms are now available fresh. Dried mushrooms can be stored indefinitely.

CHINESE CABBAGE ··· (Bok Choy) a vegetable with a white stem and dark green leaf. Sold in most grocery stores and Asian markets.

CELERY CABBAGE ··· Leafy light green cabbage also known as Chinese cabbage or napa. This vegetable has a sweeter taste than the bok choy.

CHILIES ··· The small green chilies are the most popular chilies used in Thai cooking (known as prig kee noo). These chilies are very hot and the amount used in each recipe is determined by individual preference. Other less hot varieties can be substituted. Chilies can be made less hot by removing the seeds.

COCONUT CREME ··· The thick top layer of a can of coconut milk.

COCONUT MILK ··· Coconut milk is made by grating the meat of the mature fresh coconut and combining it with hot water and squeezing through a filter to extract the liquid. The resulting liquid is the coconut milk most preferred for cooking. A second repeated process results in a thinner coconut milk used mainly for cooking other recipes requiring less coconut flavor. The clear liquid in the center of a young coconut is referred to as coconut water and is usually not used in cooking but just for drinking. Coconut milk can be purchased in cans.

CILANTRO ··· The leafy green parsley plant often referred to as Chinese parsley. Coriander is the seeds and cilantro is the leaf portion. An essential ingredient in Thai cooking.

CORIANDER SEED (DRY) ··· Available as small brown seeds. An essential ingredient in Thai cuisine. Each portion of the parsley plant has a very distinctive flavor and use.

CUMIN ··· An essential spice powder used in the making of some Thai curries and chicken or beef satay. If using seeds, roasting before grinding imparts a fuller flavor.

CURRY PASTE ··· These curry blends are used in making the various Thai curries.

GREEN ··· A blend of chilies, garlic, cilantro and lemon grass.

MUSSAMUN ··· A blend of dried red chilies, onions, coriander and other spices and herbs.

RED ··· A blend of chili peppers, garlic, lemon grass, cilantro, galanga and onions.

YELLOW ··· A blend of dried red chilies, lemon grass, galanga, garlic and other spices and herbs.

CURRY POWDER ··· A blend of many different spices used in the making of curries and marinades.

EGGPLANT ··· The Thai eggplant is the size of a pea. Other varieties of eggplant can be used. Cut to the appropriate size and use as directed in the recipes.

FIVE SPICE POWDER ··· A blend of five different spices including fennel seeds, cinnamon, cloves, ginger and star anise. It is used in some marinades.

FISH SAUCE ··· A sauce made from salted fish. This is the basic sauce used in Thai cooking. There are many varieties of fish sauce. Some are made from shrimp, anchovy and squid. It will keep indefinitely on the shelf.

GALANGA ··· A rhizome similar in appearance to ginger root. It has a different flavor and is generally sliced. Available fresh, dried or in powdered dried form.

GARLIC ··· A main ingredient in Thai cooking. Always use fresh garlic, not powder.

GINGER ROOT ··· A rhizome of the ginger plant. Young ginger has a very translucent skin, the mature ginger has a brown skin which should be peeled before using. Ginger imparts hotness and flavor to the food.

KAFFIR LIME LEAVES ··· The leaves of the kaffir lime. It has a very unique fragrance. It is available dried and sometimes fresh. Use in recipes as directed.

KAFFIR LIME SKIN ··· The skin of the kaffir lime. Only the skin is used in cooking.

KRACHAI ··· A rhizome similar to ginger root. Also known as "lesser ginger." It resembles small fingers extending from a main stem. Krachai is found whole, frozen, and dried as a powder. It is used in some Thai curries.

LEMON GRASS ··· A tall, strong, graceful grass found in Thailand and other warm weather countries. The plant has a tough fibrous stem with a very delicate refreshing aroma resembling that of lemons. Restaurants with the same name possess the same qualities. Free soul, not containable with a fresh spirit all its own.

LIME ··· Thai limes are smaller, stronger and much juicier than other limes. Fresh lime juice is preferred for all recipes.

(kaffir) ··· This lime has a bumpy outer skin and only the skin is used. The juice of this lime is seldom used in cooking.

GLOSSARY

LIME LEAVES ··· The leaves of the kaffir lime plant. The leaves impart a delicate fresh distinct flavor to the dish. No substitution. Fresh kaffir lime leaves are preferred but dried kaffir lime leaves may be used.

MINT LEAVES ··· The fresh leaves of mint. Used in recipes to impart refreshing aroma.

MUSHROOM ··· Fresh button mushrooms are most often found in grocery stores. Slice or use whole as indicated in recipes.

(Black-dried) These mushrooms must be soaked in warm water to soften. Rinse and then use in recipes as required. Keeps indefinitely on shelf.

OIL ··· Use a quality vegetable oil such as corn oil for the recipes in this book unless another oil is indicated.

ONION (GREEN) ··· Also known as spring onions. Both the green and white parts are used in cooking or for garnishing.

YELLOW ··· Large bulb onion readily available in most stores.

OYSTER SAUCE ··· A savory sauce made from oyster extract. Usually sold in bottles and keeps for several months in the refrigerator.

PALM SUGAR ··· The sap of the palm tree. The liquid is reduced to form a very thick syrup similar in flavor to brown sugar and molasses.

PAPAYA (GREEN) ··· An unripe papaya. Peel and shred to be used in green papaya salad. The ripe fruit is eaten fresh.

PEANUTS ··· Fresh peanuts are shelled and then blanched to remove the skin. Roast in oven at 350°F (175°C) until golden brown. Use as directed in recipe. Peanuts can be ground using a blender or food processor which only requires a few seconds. Grind to a coarse stage or it will turn into peanut butter. Use in cooking or in the making of peanut sauce.

PRESERVED TURNIPS ··· Sliced turnips preserved in salt. Sold in most Asian groceries.

PEPPERCORN (DRIED BLACK) ··· Dried seed of the pepper plant. The seeds are usually ground before using. Grind just before using for freshest flavor.

(DRIED WHITE) ··· The inner seed of the peppercorn. Usually sold in ground form. Imparts a different flavor from the black pepper.

RICE ··· The staple food of Thailand. Long grain rice is preferred. Jasmine rice is a variety of long grain rice which when cooked has an aroma of Jasmine.

(GLUTINOUS RICE) Or sticky rice is also called sweet rice. It is often used in the making of desserts. There are many varieties of Thai sweet rice. Some are steamed and served as the staple of a meal.

RICE NOODLE ··· Noodles made from ground rice flour. These noodles come in various forms from dried to fresh. Some resemble sheets which are steamed in layers and sold fresh. Some noodles are sold dried which come in different thickness and length. Dried rice noodles must be soaked in water before cooking.

ROYAL SAUCE (Grand Palace Foods brand) ··· A very popular sauce available in all United States grocery stores on the west coast, soon to be available nationwide. This sauce developed by Chef Rut which is very similar to a sweet and sour sauce but with much more flavor. It is a delicious accompaniment to any meat or vegetable dish. Also it can be used as a salad dressing. In the future, the sauce will be available internationally.

SHALLOTS ··· Resemble onions in flavor but have a much more delicate taste. A favorite ingredient in Thai recipes. If not available, substitute bulb yellow onions.

SHRIMP PASTE ··· A very thick dried paste made from salted shrimp. It has a very pungent strong flavor but becomes more mellow when cooked. Stores indefinitely in a tightly sealed jar.

SOMEN ··· Thin white noodles made from wheat flour. The Japanese variety is preferred. Do not overcook these noodles. Boil only for approximately 5 minutes and then rinse. Use as directed in recipe.

SOY SAUCE (REGULAR) ··· Made from salted fermented soy beans. Fish sauce is used extensively in Thai cooking instead of soy sauce to impart saltiness to most recipes.

(SWEET) ··· A thicker darker and sweeter soy sauce. Used in recipes to impart flavor and color.

STICKY RICE ··· Refer to rice.

STRAW MUSHROOMS ··· Small mushrooms

SUGAR (COCONUT) ··· Refer to palm sugar.

SWAMP CABBAGE (PUG BOONG) ··· A vegetable very similar to spinach. Available in most Asian groceries. Spinach is a good substitute.

TAMARIND ··· The long brown large bean shaped fruit of the tamarind tree. The dried form is used to impart sourness to a recipe.

TAPIOCA (SAKOO) ··· The flour made from tapioca. Tapioca starch or pearls are used to make desserts and appetizers.

TOFU ··· The curd made from soybean milk. *Tofu* is usually sold as a white 4 inch (10cm) block. Fresh *tofu* should be kept in water and lasts only a few days. To make fried *tofu*, allow most of the water to drain and deep fry in hot oil until the outer surface is golden brown. The block can also be cut into smaller cubes and then deep fried until golden brown. Use in recipes as directed.

THAI CHILIES (PRIG KEE NOO) ··· Small green chilies available at Asian groceries. These chilies are very hot and give Thai cuisine the distinctive fire. Substitute with jalapeno or serrano chilies.

TURMERIC ··· Resembles ginger root in appearance but not in flavor.Dried turmeric powder is more readily available in most Asian groceries.

WHITE PEPPER ··· Refer to pepper.

INDEX